Harps Unhung

Praising God in the Midst of Captivity

Eileen G. Anderson
&
Vicki J. Anderson

WESTBOW·
PRESS
A DIVISION OF THOMAS NELSON
& ZONDERVAN

In Loving Memory of
Eileen Gayle Anderson
1946–2013

Contents

Special Thanks

Special thanks to my dad, Jeff Anderson, who took the photograph on the front cover. This is the view from out of the window of our family cabin in Northern Minnesota where mom (his wife) wrote many of the poems contained within this book.

Special thanks to Joe Dunlap for lending his amazing artistic abilities to this project. Thank you, Joe, for the beautiful front-cover design. I pray that the Lord will continue to use your gifts for his glory.

Very special thanks to Lorry Sutherland whose enthusiasm for this project was used by God to bring this project to completion. Mom left many unfinished writing projects behind when she died. The reason this one made it to publication owes, in large part, to Lorry's prayers and encouragement. Thank you.

Special thanks to Viola Jacobson Berg, author of the exemplary book, *Pathways for the Poet*, from which most of the poetry forms used by Eileen herein were gleaned.

Special thanks to Terry Clitheroe, web host of the exemplary website The Poet's Garrett, from which most of the poetry forms used by Vicki herein were gleaned.

Preface

This poetry project was the vision of my mother, Eileen. She began work in 1992; her first poem being "Psalm 100." I am not entirely sure what first triggered her idea to write an entire collection of poetry; though a letter in her writing files seem to indicate that a poetry contest planted, perhaps, the initial seed.

She spoke of her psalm poem project often, frequently texting or emailing me to tell me when she had completed another, how many she had completed, and how many she had left to write. Through the years, her number of completed poems went from one in 1992 to seventy-five in 2013.

A Stage 3B ovarian cancer diagnosis in 2008 did little to slow her down. She continued to joyfully hope and dream and bring her vision of these poems into fruition through eighty-plus rounds of chemo, forty-plus rounds of radiation, five surgeries, countless hospital stays, various tests and procedures, and round-the-clock chronic pain.

The last week of her life, she lay in bed (many times passed out from the strong pain meds she was on) unable to write, but gripping a pen in her hand, fast asleep, with her Bible and poetry notebook on her lap. Two or three days before she died, her sister-in-law (my aunt) asked her, "Are you anxious to be free of this world?"

Mom replied, "No, I want to live. I have things left to do. I want to finish my psalm poems."

The Lord had other plans.

After the funeral, I brought Mom's (extremely organized!) poetry files home with me and began to pray over the possibility of completing the project. It sounded very romantic—a daughter taking up the mantle of her deceased mother and finishing her manuscript—but was I up for such a task? The Lord had given this vision to her, not me, and while I considered myself to be a writer, I never considered myself to be a poet, and attempting to write my first psalm poem in April 2013 only further evidenced that I was not! After two poems, I shelved the project, believing it was not my calling, but I prayed and said, "Lord, if you want me to finish this project, equip me to do so."

About a month passed, and my joyful, independent life began to crumble. One night, I cried out aloud to the Lord, "God, what is happening? *What are you doing?*" And the still, small voice in my head replied with perfect ease and calm, "I am making you a psalmist."

In the wake of my mom's death, I also lost my job, my apartment, and several dear friends. With each new loss, I would grab my pen and pour out all of the agonizing emotions of loss, hopelessness, despair, anxiety, and abysmal loneliness—writing psalm poems at the exact moments that my heart was shattering.

Every single poem contained in this volume was written with the ink of cancer, chemo, radiation, fear, physical pain, loss, death, and heartache. Even at this very moment, penning this preface, many of the heartaches of the last year have not been resolved— no "silver lining" has appeared to ease the sorrow of all of the losses or to answer the question, "Why?" But I do have this one consolation: through it all, by the grace of God, I did not hang up my harp.

By the rivers of Babylon, we sat and wept when we remembered Zion. There on the poplars we hung our harps, for there our captors asked us for songs, our tormentors demanded songs of joy; they said, "Sing us one of the songs of Zion!" How can we sing the songs of the LORD while in a foreign land? (Psalm 137:1–3)

Mom did not hang up her harp, either. Even up to the last week of her life, she kept reaching for her psalm poem notebook. In words like Job, I heard her tell many people in her last days, "The Lord gave me sixty-two years of joy and prosperity; will I curse him if the last five years are hard?" Even once exiled to the Babylon of cancer and death, the strains of her harp could be heard—indeed, can still be heard in the pages of this book.

Our vision for this poetry project was not ultimately to rewrite the psalms, to find 150 poetry forms, or even to get a book published. Our vision for this book of poetry is that hurting, hopeless saints, in the very midst of the furnace of affliction, would, despite all perceived silence from God and feelings abandonment, believe that just above their heads, seen only by the eyes of faith, is an unfurled banner, flapping wildly in the storms of heartache and suffering, its embroidered letters spelling out, "Love! My banner over you is LOVE!"

Or, in Mom's own words, "When my husband and I lost our first daughter, the psalms comforted me. When three more babies miscarried, the psalms healed my broken heart. When our second daughter was born with massive birth defects, the psalms encouraged me to live a holy life despite disappointments. When our grown son turned to drugs and a dissolute lifestyle, the psalms modeled how to dispel fear when life spins out of control. As I read, meditate, and memorize the psalms, my needs are met, and I am led to worship a loving and merciful Lord. It is my keen desire to help other hurting and hungry people discover the beauty and wisdom waiting for them in the psalms."

Sovereign, loving, almighty God of the universe, I pray for everyone holding this book in their hands. When they put it down, I pray that they would take up their harps and sing. Be glorified, O God, I pray, for you alone are worthy to receive glory, and honor, and praise, even during the darkest, most bitter seasons of our lives. Give them hope that after they have suffered a little while, you will rescue with your righteous right arm. Turn their dirges into shouts of praise. Be glorified! In Jesus' name. Amen.

A Note to the Reader

While each of the poems in this volume can "stand alone," each poem was written as an homage to the original psalm to which it corresponds in number. While the reader can understand the overall theme of each poem without reading the original psalm, much deeper meaning and beauty will be gleaned if read side by side with the corresponding biblical psalm.

Psalm 1
Ottava Rima

The child of God who does not seek his friends *Don't let Satan deceive you*
among the wicked shall be greatly blessed.
Delightedly he reads and apprehends
the Law, wherein he finds his joy and rest.
The wicked are like chaff, their day soon ends,
while he who loves the Lord receives the best.
The wicked only flounder, then they die;
the righteous rest beneath God's watchful eye. *yes.*

Psalm 2
Adagem

BLESSED are those who seek the Lord, who
ARE cognizant of him who sits enthroned.
ALL earthly kings and rulers plot in vain
WHO take their stand against the Holy One.
TAKE care, for God in heaven laughs in scorn.
REFUGE in the Son alone can quell his wrath.
IN fear, bow down and kiss the Son, revere
HIM who holds the nations in his hand.

Psalm 3
Bridges

How many are the foes that rise to conquer me.
"His God will not deliver him," they shout in glee;
      "His God is dead!"
But You, O Lord, lift up my head; you are my shield,
you answer when I cry aloud and yield
      my fear and dread.

I sleep in peace and wake because the Lord sustains.
Though thousands draw against me and my courage wanes,
      he grants me rest.
Arise, O Lord, and strike down all my enemies.
Deliv'rance comes from God; he hears; he sees;
      his own are blessed.

Psalm 4
Dionol

O answer me, I call to you, give me relief
from my distress, draw near, you are my righteous God.
Be merciful to me and hear my prayer; how long,
O men, will you turn glory into shame? I groan.
The Lord has set apart the godly for his own;
sin not, be silent, trust in God, lift up your song.
My heart is filled with joy while in this world I trod.
I sleep in peace and rest within this strong belief,
you are my righteous God.

Psalm 5
Rondel

Let all who take refuge in you be glad,
      let all sing for joy who delight in you.
      I cry in the morning when day is new.
Give ear to my words, for my heart is sad.
You hate those who in cloaks of sin are clad,
      but mercy you give to the humble few.
Let all who take refuge in you be glad,
      let all sing for joy who delight in you.

The hearts of the wicked are guilty-clad,
      their throats, open graves, from which evils spew.
      Declare they are guilty, their sins review,
but bless those who love you, your favor add,
let all who take refuge in you be glad,
      let all sing for joy who delight in you.

Psalm 6
Dowson

All night I groan and flood my bed with weeping.
       I drench my couch with tears;
my eyes grow dim with fears rather than sleeping
       as morning nears.

How long before you note my anguished sorrow?
       My eyes grow weak with woes;
accept my prayer for mercy, and tomorrow
       turn back my foes.

Psalm 7
Zanze

My shield is God Most High who saves,
who spares me from those who pursue.
As enemies prepare my grave,
I find my refuge, Lord, in you.

My shield is God Most High,
who overtakes my foe
in answer to my cry
and brings the wicked low.

My shield is God;
express your wrath
on those who plod
an evil path.

My shield
is him who paves
my way with peaceful yield.
My shield is God Most High who saves.

Psalm 8
Lyrelle

O Lord, our Lord,
majestic is your name.
From infant lips, you are adored,
your glory, set above all else, proclaim.

I see the sky,
your artistry displayed;
then what is man, and what am I
that you love me above all that you've made!

Your flocks, your herds,
you give to man to tame.
In honor, crown him by your words.
O Lord, our Lord, majestic is your name!

Psalm 9
Villanelle

You judge the world in righteousness
      and turn back all my enemies;
with thankful heart, your name I bless.

You slay the wicked who oppress
      the ones who follow your decrees.
You judge the world in righteousness.

The needy cry in their distress,
      you hearken to their fearful pleas;
with thankful heart, your name I bless.

The nations that do not confess
      that God is God shall find no ease;
you judge the world in righteousness.

While those who love your name shall press
      close to Your side on bended knees;
with thankful heart, your name I bless.

Arise, O Lord, in mightiness
      And govern nations as you please;
you judge the world in righteousness.
With thankful heart, your name I bless.

Psalm 10
Stellar

O Lord, why do you stand away
and hide yourself when troubles threat?
The wicked hunts the weak like prey,
with schemes, he snares them in his net.
He sneers at God with prideful ravings,
he boasts of all his lustful cravings,
  he leaves no room
for thoughts of God within to bloom.

The laws of God are far from him,
yet everything he does succeeds.
His mouth is filled up to the brim
with lies and threats of evil deeds.
He waits, his eyes alert and gleaming
to trap the helpless by his scheming;
  he laughs in glee
and tells himself, "God does not see."

Arise, O Lord, lift up your hand!
Do not forget the frail, the weak,
the one who can no longer stand
against the foe, nor run, nor speak.
O listen to the victims crying,
spare those who helplessly are dying,
  then heed their cry,
that men may no more terrify.

Psalm 11
Cavatina

How can you say to me, flee like a bird
      and fly away?
For even now the wicked bend their bows
      against their prey;
foundations crumble. Where then should we go?
      To God alone,
who hates the wicked and decides their fate
      upon his throne.
The wicked will be brought down in disgrace,
but those who love the Lord will see his face.

Psalm 12
Sevenelle

O Lord, where are the faithful ones,
the godly fathers, righteous sons?
They flatter with their lying lips;
deceit spews forth, and boasting drips
from hearts consumed by sinful grips.
The Lord declares, "I will protect
the weak, the needy, my select."

But when, O Lord, will you arise
and cut off flattery and lies?
When what is adm'rable is vile,
the wicked strut in proud denial,
not knowing what they love is guile.
The Lord declares, "I will protect
the weak, the needy, my select."

Psalm 13
Octave

How long, O Lord, will you conceal
your face from me and let me dwell
with thoughts that wound and will not heal
within my heart, my private hell?
Give light to me or else I die;
I plead with you who reigns above,
I sing to you, O hear my cry;
I trust in your unfailing love!

Psalm 14
De Tabley

The fool says in his heart, "There is no God."
       They are corrupt and vile,
their evilness is masked by a façade—
       a pompous, empty smile.

The Lord from heaven looks down onto men;
       do any understand?
Do any seek to know or hear again
       all that the Lord has planned?

But God is present with the righteous ones—
       a refuge for the poor;
the Lord restores the fortunes of his sons;
       be glad forevermore!

Psalm 15
Spenserian Stanza

Who upon hills holy—live with the Lord?
Who may dwell within your sanctuary?
He whose walk is blameless, fully godward,
he who with his whole heart speaks truthfully,
he who treats his neighbors well and humbly,
he who honors those who fear the Godhead,
he who lends his money, sharing freely,
he who firmly keeps all oaths that he's said,
He who does these things, in truth, shall be rewarded.

Psalm 16
Russell

You have assigned my portion and my place,
my heritage is beautiful and sure.
In humbleness, my bound'ry lines I trace;
      you've made my lot secure.

I praise the Lord who counsels me at night,
I set the Lord before me all my days;
therefore, I'll not be shaken nor know fright,
      I rest secure always.

You have made known to me the righteous way,
eternal pleasures are at your right hand;
you fill my life with joy from day to day;
      I rest in all you've planned.

Psalm 17
Arkaham Ballad

O hear my cry, my righteous plea,
give ear unto my plight.
It does not rise from lips that lie;
I'm vindicated in your eye,
for you see what is right.

For you see what is right and good;
you probe my heart at night;
you test but find no wrong within.
I have resolved my mouth won't sin;
I'm blameless in your sight.

I'm blameless in your sight, for I
hold firmly to your Law;
my steps have held on to your path,
and so, I never see your wrath.
I look to you in awe.

I look to you in awe, O Lord,
I hide beneath your wing.
Keep me the apple of your eye,
destroy the wicked, nullify
all those who spurn the King.

All those who spurn the King are doomed;
rise up and bring them low.
This fleeting life is their reward;
cast down the wicked with your sword,
O save me from my foe!

O save me from my foe, from men
who seek my full disgrace.
Then I, in righteousness, will see;
when I awake, my fear will flee,
for I will see your face.

Psalm 18
Chant Royal

I love the Lord, my strength and my delight,
my refuge and my rock when I despair,
my horn of salvation in every plight;
there is no other god who can compare;
when foes attacked and filled my heart with dread,
it was to him, my fortress, that I fled;
I ask him now, again, to overthrow
my enemies who cause me so much woe
and save me that I might not suffer shame;
reveal his worth, let all his glory show;
I will sing praises to his holy name!

The cords of death entangled me in fright;
destruction coiled about me like a snare;
the grave reached out to claim me in the night,
but I cried to the Lord, "O hear my prayer!"
He heard my cry, he lifted up his head;
he stood at heaven's doorway and there spread
the curtains of the Earth and came below
to rescue me from every mighty foe;
the mountains shook, the earth quaked in its frame
as he reached down and brought the wicked low;
I will sing praises to his holy name.

He bent down from on high and showed his might;
he drew me out from waters deep, and there
defeated ev'ry foe without a fight;
he put me in a spacious place of care;
he rescued me, no blood of mine was shed;
my hands are clean, he took my place instead
and did for me more than I'll ever know;
I'm righteous in his eyes, to him I owe
all gratitude for ev'ry breath I claim;
I will sing praises everywhere I go;
I will sing praises to his holy name.

God is faithful; he's blameless, pure, and right;
my ev'ry burden he will gladly bear;
he turns my days of darkness into light;
he gives me ev'ry blessing as my share;
and when my enemies desire me dead,
follow faded footsteps from places fled,
he cares for me, he keeps my lamp aglow;
abundant blessings rain and overflow;
it seems my peace and joy must be his aim
as he has loved and cared for me; and so
I will sing praises to his holy name!

God saves those who are humble and contrite,
but those who rise against him, he'll not spare,
for all those who are wicked in his sight,
he will subdue; let all his foes beware.
He gives me feet like deer so where I tread
my steps are firm, I boldly march ahead;
I crush my foes; they run in fear although
I never shoot an arrow from my bow.
I praise my God! To him be all the fame,
to him may anthems sing and trumpets blow;
I will sing praises to his holy name!

The Lord lives! May all my worship flow
from lips and heart aflame with love to show
the nations that he's worthy of his fame;
I'll praise the Lord so all the world will know;
I will sing praises to his holy name!

Psalm 19
Sonnet

The skies proclaim the glory of the Lord
in thund'rous shouts and luminary voice
that all the nations, tribes, and tongues observe
the throbbing language of the glory-chord.
The sun, he holds in harness by his choice,
then sets it free to trace the cosmic curve.
His perfect law revives the soul, and wise
his statutes make; his precepts shower hearts
with joy; his luminous commands give light.
His ordinances, valued as a prize,
are righteous; yet a warning they impart.
In keeping them, alone, is there delight.
Forgive my sins, both hidden and abhorred,
accept my worship and my love, O Lord.

Psalm 20
Dorsimbra

The Lord will answer us when in distress;
help from his sanctuary will he send;
our humble offerings to Spirit bless,
and all our hoped-for plans will he commend.

> We will shout for joy,
> we will lift our banners high
> in the name of our God
> when we see victory!

Some trust in horses, some in chariots;
they are brought to their knees, they swiftly fall;
but we trust in the name of the Lord our God;
the Lord will answer us when in distress.

Psalm 21
Quatern

The king rejoices in your might!
On your great strength I will depend.
My enemies are yours to fight;
how great my joy when you defend.

Your strength I cannot apprehend;
the king rejoices in your might!
Your majesty will never end;
to trust in you is my delight.

My enemies are seized with fright,
your righteous wrath on them descend;
the king rejoices in your might!
Your strength they cannot comprehend.

O may my praise to you ascend.
Your strength and glory I recite;
your power over all transcends;
the king rejoices in your might!

Psalm 22
Sestina

My God, why are you far from saving ME
and why forsake me when to you I CRY?
All day and night I groan, I have no STRENGTH,
yet you are still the one in whom I TRUST;
our fathers called to you and they were SAVED;
you are the Holy One enthroned in PRAISE.

I am a worm and worthy not of PRAISE;
the people sneer and shake their heads at ME;
"Trust in your Lord," they mock, "and then be SAVED."
Do not be far from me, O God, I CRY,
for at my birth, in you I placed my TRUST;
no one can help but God; you are my STRENGTH.

Surrounding me are bulls of awesome STRENGTH,
while lions lurk and roar in prideful PRAISE;
my bones are out of joint, who can I TRUST?
My heart of wax has melted within ME,
my strength is gone, yet to the Lord I CRY;
though I lie in the dust, I will be SAVED.

When evil men enshroud me, I'll be SAVED;
though dogs surround me and I lose my STRENGTH,
my help is not far off; Lord, hear my CRY,
deliver me and I will give You PRAISE;
my life is in your hands, O rescue ME,
you are my strength, in you I place my TRUST.

He listened to my cry, this God I TRUST,
and from the mouths of lions I've been SAVED;
I will declare what he has done for ME;
so call on him, O you of little STRENGTH,
and give him all the honor, all the PRAISE;
he will not turn from you, he'll hear your CRY.

This is my theme of praise, O Lord, I CRY;
I will fulfill my vows, a sacred TRUST;
all those who seek the Lord will give him PRAISE;
let all the nations who bow down be SAVED,
for you hold all dominions by your STRENGTH;
I will proclaim what you have done for ME.

So now hear ME and listen to my CRY;
the Lord is your STRENGTH, give him all your TRUST,
then you will be SAVED, and God will get PRAISE.

Psalm 23
Quintanelle

My Shepherd is the Lord. I have no needs
as I lie down in peace where'ere he leads,
        by streams serene
      or pastures lush and green,
he lifts, restores my soul; on him I lean.

And though I walk through valleys dark with death,
as horrors haunt my soul and steal my breath,
        I will not fear
      for you are ever near,
the comfort of your rod and staff are dear.

You set a place for me among my foes,
anoint my head with oil; my cup o'erflows;
        You follow me
      with love beyond degree,
and in your house I'll dwell eternally.

Psalm 24
Marianne

God made the earth
and all that dwells therein;
he founded it by his own worth
and granted each
its birth.

Who may ascend
his high and holy hill?
Whose hearts are clean may apprehend
the Lord who will
befriend.

O ancient doors
and gates, lift up your heads,
the King of Glory evermore
comes that you may
adore.

Who is this King?
The Lord strong and mighty,
the King of Glory, praises bring
to him; rejoice
and sing!

Psalm 25
Sestennelle

I lift my soul
to Him who will console,
to God in whom my hope finds full reward;
teach me your ways,
forget my sin-filled days,
remember me with mercy, O my Lord.

Upright is he
who teaches his decree;
the humble he forgives; there's no more shame.
He guides the man
who seeks to know his plan;
the Lord confides in those who fear his name.

Lord, turn to me
and set my anguish free;
the troubles of my heart have multiplied;
I hope in you,
secure in all you do.
I find my rest and refuge by your side.

Psalm 26
Octodil

Vindicate me,
be merciful;
while others bribe and scheme,
I lead a blameless life,
I walk steadfastly in your truth,
I speak of all your awesome deeds;
test me, then redeem me,
and I will sing your praise.

Psalm 27
Veltanelle

The Lord is my light and my salvation,
      of whom then shall I fear?
The Lord is my firm stronghold where I run
      when evil men appear;
when enemies attack me, they will fall.
My hope is in the Lord, on him I call.

One thing I ask, this one thing I desire:
      that all my earthly days
my eyes would gaze on him whom I admire.
      His beauty I would praise;
with shouts of joy, my sacrifice I bring.
I will make music to my Lord and King.

Be merciful to me and hear my call,
      attend me when I speak,
do not forsake me, do not let me fall;
      your face, Lord, I will seek.
My confidence rests sure upon this chord,
that I will see the goodness of the Lord.

Psalm 28
Octosyllabic Couplets

To you I call, O Lord my Rock,
do not seal up your ears and mock

my heart's desire to be heard;
for if my cry should be deferred,

I'll lose all hope, my pleas shall quit,
like those who've gone down to the pit.

When you drag cruel men away,
who speak with charm while hearts betray,

O let me not be found with them
whose wicked works you must condemn;

repay them for their evil deeds,
who show no honor for your creeds.

I praise the Lord who heeds my cry,
I sing my thanks for his supply,

for he has heard and he has blessed
and made salvation manifest

to those whose hope no fear can dim,
to those who place their trust in Him.

Psalm 29
Terza Rima

Ascribe to the Lord, O you mighty ones,
ascribe to him glory and strength and praise,
for he is due honor; let all Earth's sons

bow down and worship him all of their days.
The voice of the Lord strips the forests bare,
Mount Hermon skips like a calf 'neath his gaze;

the voice of the Lord strikes with lightning flare,
the Deserts of Kadesh shudder and shake.
Let all the Earth fear, all people beware

as Cedars of Lebanon twist and break;
the voice of God thunders o'er everything
while waters and mountains tremble and quake.

Let all the Earth worship, rejoice, and sing;
the Lord sits enthroned, our eternal King.

Psalm 30
Duodora

Sing to the Lord!
Who spared me from the pit,
saved me from the grave,
raised me from the depths,
healed me when I called;
for his anger lasts only a moment,
but his favor persists for a lifetime.

Sing to the Lord!
I praise his holy name!
My heart sings my thanks,
my lips can't be still
for he is my God;
my tears have turned into dances of joy,
my mountain stands firm, my joy is sublime.

Psalm 31
Arnold

O Lord, in you I hide,
deliver me from shame,
come quickly to my side,
preserve your righteous name;
redeem me, free me from the trap that's set for me.

Though some to idols cling,
my trust is in you, Lord,
in gladness I will sing,
my plight, you've not ignored;
you've set my feet instead in places wide and free.

My neighbors turn and flee,
my friends treat me with dread,
like broken pottery;
I'm looked on as though dead;
be merciful to me, O Lord, in my distress.

My times are in your hands,
I shelter in your sight,
deliver me from bands
of foes who cause me fright;
be strong, O saints, our hope is in his faithfulness.

Psalm 32
Chain Verse

Rejoice in the Lord, you upright in heart,
rejoice and be glad, you righteous, and sing;
your sins are forgiven, in whole, not part,
blessed are all those who rejoice in the King.

Rejoice and be glad, you righteous, and sing,
confess to the Lord while he may be found,
for when I kept silent and did not bring
my guilt to the Lord, my grief was profound.

Confess to the Lord while he may be found,
acknowledge iniquity, seek his face
before mighty waters cover the ground;
he will forgive and be your hiding place.

Acknowledge iniquity, seek his face,
may his unfailing love to you impart,
may his songs of deliverance be your brace;
rejoice in the Lord, you upright in heart!

Psalm 33
Herrick

You righteous ones, let voices trill,
you upright, shout his praises,
with loud instruments, play with skill,
for all God's work amazes.

He formed the heavens with his breath,
he stores the seas in vessels;
the Earth, in all its length and breadth,
close to his heart he nestles.

The word of God is true and right,
his justice, all-prevailing;
his righteousness is his delight,
his love is never-failing.

Let all the people, small and grand,
stand at his feet, revering;
for he will do all he has planned
to all nations not fearing.

He sees from heaven all mankind,
his eyes are on the trusting,
but he who trusts in his own mind,
God loathes and finds disgusting.

So wait in hope, God is our shield,
our heart in him rejoices;
we trust in him, our lives we yield;
let's sing with joyful voices!

Psalm 34
Acrostic

My soul will boast in the Lord, for I
Yearn to exalt his name.

Seeking to worship, we magnify
Our Lord and shout his fame;
Utterly trusting in him, we cry,
Longing to shun our shame.

We taste and see that the Lord is good,
In all, he meets our need;
Lions grow weak, while saints from childhood
Learn to ask and to plead.

By trusting in the Lord as we should,
Our needs he does exceed.
Ask of me, for I'm longing to teach:
Seek the Lord while you may,
Test to see if there's lies in your speech.

In evil, turn away,
Near to us is the Lord's loving reach

To help without delay.
He is close to those with broken hearts,
Each crushed soul, he revives,

Lost is the wicked, his soul departs,
Obliged to not survive.
Refuge is for whom God sets apart,
Devoted, righteous lives.

Psalm 35

Latova

Lord, contend with all my foes,
fight for me, come to my aid,
brandish javelin and blade,
shame all those who seek my harm,
rescue me from all alarm,
save me with your strong right arm,
snare them in the net they made,
heal me from their deadly blows,
Lord, your goodness overflows.

Ruthless people question me,
slander buffets without end,
hateful mocking from a friend;
be not silent, Lord, I pray,
rise to my defense this day,
let my lips forever say,
"Hail the Lord who will defend,
shout for joy, he's set me free;
praise his name eternally."

Psalm 36
Sacred Signia

The wickedness of man exemplifies
      his sinful state;
there is no fear of God before his eyes;
      his crowning trait
is flattering himself so that he feels
      that he is great.
Deceitful words his true intent reveals;
a sinful course of life is what appeals;
he ceases to do good and to be wise;
an evil plot is all that satisfies.

Your faithfulness, O Lord, reaches the sky,
      O priceless love;
your righteousness is like a mountain high
      that soars above;
your justice flows like waters of the deep
      in truth thereof;
we refuge 'neath your wings wherein you keep
both man and beast who shelter there and sleep;
we eat and drink from your immense supply;
our every need you richly satisfy.

Psalm 37
Lavelle

Of evil men you need not fret;
just live your life without regret.

Those who do wrong will fade away
like blooms that only live a day.
Commit to God your will, your way.

Refrain from anger, wait, be still,
the wicked thrive only until
like smoke, they vanish by God's will.

Better a mite and righteousness
than wealth that wicked men possess;
all disappear but holiness.

When God approves, the righteous stand,
the Lord upholds them with his hand.

The man whose mind on God is set
will find his every need is met.

Psalm 38
LuVailean Sonnet

O Lord, do not rebuke me in your wrath;
       your discipline,
like arrows, pierces me along the path
       that leads to sin.
My guilt has overwhelmed me, I'm brought low,
       I'm filled with pain;
my loathsome sin has crushed me like a foe,
       my strength is slain.
My longings are not hidden from your ears;
       O hear my plea;
forgive my sin and wipe away my tears;
       draw near to me.
Come quickly to my side; Lord, hear my prayer.
Do not forsake me in my deep despair.

Psalm 39
Tercets with Identical Refrain

I will keep my tongue and watch o'er my ways;
I will muzzle my mouth so it obeys;
but anger grows hot, my silence betrays.
       How fleeting is my life.

The days of a man are but a mere handbreadth;
in vain he gains wealth, then leaves all in death;
his life, like a moth, is only a breath.
       How fleeting is my life.

O Lord, hear my prayer, listen to my cry;
be not deaf to my weeping, mortify
the sin that I bear lest I should die.
       How fleeting is my life.

Psalm 40
Abercrombie

I waited for the Lord; he heard my cry,
he lifted me out of the pit
and set my feet upon a rock whereby
      I am now firmly standing.

He put within my mouth a song of praise
that others hear and benefit;
blessed is the one who trusts the Lord always
      and treasures his commanding.

Many are the wonders our God has done,
no one can count all that he's planned;
sacrifice and offerings he will shun,
      that is not his requiring.

But those who do his will, who keep his law,
who speak his truth and boldly stand,
who tell of his salvation with great awe,
      that is the Lord's desiring.

Do not withhold your mercy from me, Lord,
protect me with your truth and love,
for troubles overtake me like a horde,
      my heart, in fear, is failing.

Be pleased, O Lord, to quickly rescue me,
bend down and help me from above,
turn back and put to shame by your decree
      my foes who are assailing.

Psalm 41
Hexaduad

Come sing
to God everlasting,
who preserves my life in the land
and helps me stand.
When ill, he restores me
by his mercy.
My enemies
say I've a vile disease;
my friend betrays,
but God upholds me all my days.
To God everlasting,
come sing!

Psalm 42
Apostrophe

Why are you downcast, O my soul,
why so disturbed within me?
Praise God, my Savior and my Lord,
in him, your hope must be.
For as the deer pants for the stream,
so thirst, O soul, for God;
though night and day you feed on tears,
let mem'ry be your prod;
recall the times, O downcast soul,
we led the festive throng
up to the house of God in praise,
with shouts and joyful song.

By day the Lord directs his love,
at night, his song is mine;
and yet, O soul, you mourn as though
your death was God's design.
Your foes, O soul, oppress and taunt,
they jeer, "Where is your Lord?"
But we will cling to God, our Rock,
beloved and adored.
Why are you downcast, O my soul,
why so disturbed within me?
Praise God, my Savior and my Lord,
in him, your hope must be.

Psalm 43
De La Mare

Why must I go about mourning?
Why have you rejected me?
Bring me to your holy mountain,
        there set me free.
My delight is in your altar;
with the harp I give you praise.
My hope is in you, my Savior,
        all of my days.

Psalm 44
Donne

Our fathers spoke of deeds done in their day,
when God drove out the nations with his hand;
the peoples living there, he cast away
and gave his own possession of the land.
His love outpoured and on display
      that they might stand.

But now, we flee like sheep in disarray;
our foes who hate us, we cannot withstand;
we are a scorn to those who call us prey.
But where is God? We do not understand,
because we do not disobey
      the Lord's command.

Awake, O Lord, arise, do not delay;
do not afflict us with your reprimand;
hide not your face but help us to obey
that we may humbly follow your demand.
Lead us, O Lord, along the way
      of all you planned.

Psalm 45
Amphion

My heart is stirred, my tongue must sing;
  Gird your sword,
  Mighty Lord,
in majesty, ride forth, O King.
  Take your bride
  to your side
to reign with you in righteous peace,
  through all time,
  joy sublime;
the nations' praise will never cease.

Psalm 46
Tennyson

God says, "Be Still"

God says, "Be still," and so I will be still,
though mountains fall into the ocean floor.
I will not fear as raging waters roar
and earth gives way and crumbles at his will.
        God says, "Be still."

God says, "Be still," and so I will not fear.
While nations are distressed and kingdoms fall,
he lifts his voice; the earth melts at his call;
he ceases wars and breaks the bow and spear.
        God says, "Be still."

God says, "Be still and know that I am God.
Exalted I shall be in all the earth."
And so I shall not fear; I know his worth.
I trust in him, my refuge and my rod.
        God says, "Be still."

Psalm 47
Tanka

Shout to God with joy;
awesome is the Lord Most High
on his holy throne.
All the Earth belongs to him;
sing praise to God, sing praises.

Psalm 48
Balance

Great is the Lord and most worthy of praise
in the city of the great King,
mount of his holiness,
high and lofty
Zion.

Foes run,
they turn and flee,
for God is the fortress;
kings advance, then retreat trembling,
like ships destroyed by wind, his pow'r displays.
But we give thanks to him all of our days;
we meditate on him and sing;
he is all righteousness,
his sovereignty
begun

has won
Earth's bended knee.
Consider and confess,
tell generations following:
"Great is the Lord and most worthy of praise!"

Psalm 49
Medallion

Listen, people,
rich and poor alike, give ear:
riches without understanding
make a wealthy man a beast.
When the splendor of his house increased,
men were awed and marveled at his standing;
blessed he feels until his end draws near,
leaving all behind, he dies...
words to the wise.

Psalm 50
Triad

Look Toward the Lord!

The mighty one bids all the Earth
to hear his judgment of all men.
He comes with raging wind and fire
and summons Earth's and heaven's horde
to listen as he testifies
against mankind with one accord;
for God himself is judge of all...
　　　Look toward the Lord!

He says to those who are his own,
"I have no need of sacrifice,
I own the cattle on the hills;
I long to hear your thanks outpoured,
I'll come to you if you will call."
　　　Look toward the Lord!

But to the wicked, he declares,
"You use your mouth to speak deceit,
you slander your own mother's son,
your ev'ry action is abhorred;
so I accuse you to your face,
and my rebuke is your reward."
Consider this before you fall...
　　　Look toward the Lord!

Psalm 51
Ballade

Have mercy on me, God, cleanse me from sin
according to your kind and loving ways;
blot out all my transgressions hid within,
iniquity that plagues me all my days.
The evil you have seen in me displays
that you are justified to judge. You know
from birth I have been sinful in your gaze;
O, wash me, Lord, and make me white as snow.

Against you only has my sinning been,
for I have lived as one who disobeys,
but you desire truth from me again.
Create in me a heart of endless praise,
a steadfast spirit that in joy can raise
a song of righteousness for all I owe;
show mercy to me now, make no delays;
O, wash me, Lord, and make me white as snow.

Restore to me salvation's joy wherein
your Holy Spirit's voice of love conveys
your presence here beside me through Earth's din.
Create in me a heart that never strays,
a steadfast spirit, firm, that never sways;
let all my bones rejoice so I may show
your favor toward the broken heart that prays;
O, wash me, Lord, and make me white as snow.

Then I will show transgressors your pathways
and from my mouth my praise will overflow;
I sacrifice my heart with love ablaze;
O, wash me, Lord, and make me white as snow.

Psalm 52
Louise

O, mighty man, why do you boast of evil
when in the eyes of God, you're a disgrace?
Your tongue, a sharpened razor, plots destruction;
      all truth efface.

But God, who sees, will bring you down to ruin;
he'll snatch you up and tear you from your tent,
uproot you from among those who are living;
      your evil spent.

But I will flourish like a tree of olives,
for I will trust in God all of my days,
and in his house forever will I flourish
      and give him praise.

Psalm 53
Trench

"There is no God!" the fool says in his heart.
He is corrupt, and all his ways are vile.
      He does no good.
God searched for those his wisdom to impart,
      but no one understood.

The wicked turn from God, they never learn,
while those who trust in him are overwhelmed.
      Do they not know?
The bones of their attackers he will burn,
      their foes he'll overthrow.

O, let salvation come from Zion's shores;
let Jacob shout and Israel be glad
      and understand
when God the fortunes of his own restores
      and does all he has planned.

Psalm 54
Retournello

O God, save me;
by your might, vindicate!
Before your throne, I supplicate:
"O God, save me!"

My enemies—
ruthless men seek my breath;
self-declared gods, O, put to death
my enemies!

God, my helper,
wield your sword. Recompense
the wicked, my shield and defense:
God, my helper.

My sacrifice,
with free will, I offer:
rich praises from my soul-coffer;
my sacrifice!

O God, save me!
Lord, be my salvation!
My spirit swells with elation,
for God saved me!

Psalm 55
Rondeau

O, hear my prayer, do not ignore my plea;
O, listen to my cry and answer me;
      my heart is anguished, troubled thoughts prevail;
      my foes revile me, wicked threats assail;
because of them, I suffer endlessly.

If I had wings as doves, I'd rise and flee
to some deserted place where I'd be free;
      a shelter from the tempest and the gale;
      O, hear my prayer.

Not only enemies assault, but he,
my friend, no longer grants me loyalty.
      I call to God, who saves me when I fail,
      who ransoms me unharmed when I am frail;
bring down the wicked by your just decree;
      O, hear my prayer.

Psalm 56
Swannet

Be gracious to me, O God, midst my strife;
my enemies, they oppress and attack!
They come with sharp tongue, with noose, and with rack—
my foes come with cords to siphon my life.
All day I am crushed under oppression;
the wicked accuse—interrogating—
twisting my words like two serpents mating;
how long will you ignore their transgression?
You stayed by my side along wand'ring ways;
you stored my bitter tears in your cruet.
You set traps, then lured my foes into it;
all thanks to the Lord whose word I will praise!
Be gracious to me, O God, midst my strife;
my foes come with cords to siphon my life.

Psalm 57
Decannelle

Mercy, God, on me, have mercy.
I take refuge 'neath your wing;
save me from those who persecute,
men, whose words like arrows sting.
God, above all be exalted,
may your glory swell and sing,
for your love reaches the heavens
and your glory crowns the Earth;
let my soul well up with praises,
let my voice extol your worth.

Psalm 58
Logolilt

The wicked from the womb speak lies,
their hearts devise
mistruth;
like venom from a snake, they spew
what is not true
from youth.

Tear out their fangs, O God, destroy
their evil joy,
and then
reward the righteous and ensure
your judgment for
all men.

Psalm 59
Cycle

Save me, O God, from the vile, savage—
     see how they wait for me;
Though blameless, they hunt down, they ravage,
     they run and make ready.

Rouse your rod, God, punish all races
     that act treacherously,
who howl like hell hounds—a cur paces,
     prowling 'round the city.

Leash with laughter, muzzle flews, growling.
     With wrath and treachery,
consume cursing, lying lips, scowling,
     my God, my fortress be!

Psalm 60
Rime Couee

O God, why have you rejected;
turned your back on us—defected?
We beg of you, draw near!
The whole Earth shook, land, dissected;
tannin spewed forth and infected
our quaking hearts with fear.

Your holy ensign thwarts the spear;
your right hand grasps those you hold dear.
Our borders shall expand!
Mighty Ephraim, brave chevalier;
Courageous Judah—commandeer!
In triumph—seize the land!

But who shall lead Edom's command
to the city whose walls withstand
all of our spears and bows?
Your repudiation—remand—,
uphold us with your strong right hand
and trample down our foes!

Psalm 61
Balasi Stanza

Soul, why do you languish
on a bed of anguish?
Heart, why downcast and lowly?
Lay aside all power,
run to your strong tower,
and lean upon him wholly!
In stillness, you will sing
'neath shelter of his wing,
for he will rescue solely.

Lord, remember my vow
and your plan to endow
upon those who fear your name
a heritage of years
in exchange for our tears,
our sorrow and our shame.
May I forever be
loved by God!—Loved by thee—
two hearts beat as one aflame.

Psalm 62
Kipling

When hopes and dreams lie in state, O soul, you must learn to wait
through turmoil and violence.
There is no greater boulder than the Almighty's shoulder
'midst raging storm of silence.

How long will my name be spurned, like a lattice overturned?
On spiked tongues, their words impale.
With flattery they attack; kind speech spills over jaws, slack—
their kisses are betrayal.

Soul, you must not interlope, for God alone is your hope—
your only supplication.
O frail heart, you mustn't quake; our fortress will never shake—
God is our extrication!

phantom, an unsubstantial image

The rich, they are eidolon; all they earned, they have stolen
what could not be afforded.
But God shall come in power and with a generous dower,
his own, richly rewarded!

Psalm 63
Cyclus

O God,
you are my God;
earnestly I seek you;
my body longs for you;
my spirit thirsts
for you.
I lift
my hands in praise;
my spirit you renew;
my soul is satisfied;
my love is all
for you.

Psalm 64
Goethe Stanza

Father, soothe my fear-stained heart,

for my sorrow is immense;
my courage, it strips apart

like whitewash chipping from a fence.

Preserve my life from malice, dread,

and the ax that my foe swings;
in midst of war, make my bed

in the safe shadow of your wings.

They pith with cruel words—poison darts;

with tongues of steel, they assail;
they set traps and build ramparts,

but all their evil plots shall fail!

Flattering lips all join in song—

praises of an off-key choir;
like gnarled fingers dragged along,

catching on the strings of a lyre.

But God shall recompense their mirth—

shall cut them off at the stem;
with a word he'll spin the Earth,

'til their own arrows point back at them!

Then all of mankind shall tremble

at the Lord's wrath and tumult;
but the upright shall assemble

to praise his great name and exult!

Psalm 65
Retruecano (Glosa)

> God in Zion, receive all our reverence and fear;
> satisfy our souls in the courts of your dwelling,
> let creation sing and bow at your throne.

God in Zion, receive all our reverence and fear;
all of your laws, we avow to adhere.
We are worms in the dust; we writhe, we despair,
dragging flesh to the ear that hears our prayer.
Behold, the voices of those you have drawn near:
"God in Zion, receive all our reverence and fear!"

Satisfy our souls in the courts of your dwelling
where your righteousness rises like tides of hope swelling.
Girded with might, dressed in robes of vast powers,
your strength stills the seas and upholds terra towers.
Put this song into awe-stunned hearts, now welling:
"Satisfy our souls in the courts of your dwelling!"

Let creation sing and bow at your throne;
may the dew of your mercy be a balm to atone
dry furrows and fields where grain no longer grows,
into green pastures of joy—a harvest overflows
with wheat genuflecting beneath breezes that moan:
"Let creation sing and bow at your throne!"

Psalm 66
Pantoum

O, shout for joy to God, O earth,
sing forth the glory of his name;
his awesome deeds declare his worth;
all creatures bow, their praise proclaim.

Sing forth the glory of his name,
come see the deeds that he has done;
all creatures bow, their praise proclaim,
his awesome works excelled by none.

Come see the deeds that he has done:
he turned the sea into dry land;
his awesome works excelled by none,
his people crossed the sea on sand.

He turned the sea into dry land;
come listen, all who fear the Lord;
his people crossed the sea on sand;
we raise our praise in one accord.

Come listen, all who fear the Lord:
his awesome deeds declare his worth;
we raise our praise as one accord.
O, shout for joy to God, O earth!

Psalm 67
Blunden

May God be gracious and bless us
and make his face to shine,
that all his ways may be well-known,
salvation to all nations shown.
May all the people praise you thus,
may all the praise be thine!

You rule the peoples fair and just,
the nations joy express.
You guide the nations of the Earth.
May all the people praise your worth;
the land will yield its crops robust,
and God—our God—will bless.

Psalm 68
Ballad

Refrain
O, summon your power and show us your might,
give strength to your people that we may live right.

Sing praises to God and sing praise to his name,
extol him who rides on a cloud;
his name is the Lord, we rejoice before him,
we rejoice as we sing out loud!

God scatters his enemies, foes disappear,
as smoke blows away in the wind.
As wax melts away in the heat of the flame,
so perish those dead in their sin.

Defender of widows is God, holy God,
a father to those who have none,
while those who rebel, those who turn from the Lord,
live in a land scorched by the sun.
He led his own people through desert and hills;
the Earth shook; the sky poured down rain.

Psalm 69
Rondeau Redouble

Save me, O God, from flood and from mire;
my eyes dim watching for consummation!
Bind up my foes like tares on a pyre—
those bent to destroy my reputation.

My spirit clothed in alienation;
zeal for your house scalds my soul afire.
I crumble 'neath flaming condemnation;
save me, O God, from flood and from mire!

Sackcloth and ashes—my sole attire;
drunkards besot by intoxication,
join slurred voices in a mocking choir.
My eyes dim watching for consummation.

Your arm, O Lord, is my liberation,
and your face is my only desire.
In the midst of my humiliation,
bind up my foes like tares on a pyre.

Burn down their tents with your holy ire,
raze their camps to utter desolation.
Blot from your book and banish to fire
those bent to destroy my reputation.

I shall sing loudly in adoration;
my praises shall delight and inspire
hearts of the lowly to consecration;
this endless song shall never retire:
"Save me, O God!"

Psalm 70
Bryant

Hasten, God, to save me,
come quickly to my aid without delay;
shame those who seek my life; by your decree,
　　disgrace my foes, I pray.

But those who seek your way,
all those who love salvation, at your side,
may they in glad rejoicing always say,
　　"Let God be glorified!"

Yet, I am in great need,
and you alone are my deliverer;
come quickly, Lord, and save me, this I plead,
　　Jehovah, conqueror.

Psalm 71
Repete

Deliver me from evil men
      that I may ever give you praise.
You are my rock, my refuge when
      the wicked scorn my foe betrays.
You taught me from my youth and then
      to my old age to seek your ways.
Deliver me from evil men
      and I will ever give you praise.

No one like you has ever been;
      your righteous acts, your might amaze.
I will proclaim your deeds again
      and shout for joy throughout my days.
Deliver me from evil men,
      for I will ever give you praise.

Psalm 72
Septilla (Spanish Septet)

Give justice to the royal heir,
make his judgments both wise and fair.
     Righteousness rings from piked terrain.
Protect the poor, crush the captors
throughout endless mortal chapters.
     Bless the king like grass dank with rain
     'til lunar tears fall in despair.

Rule the Earth from topsoil to crust!
Desert tribes bow down—lick the dust!
     Kings of Earth pay tribute—render!
Bow to God, fall on your faces;
those you reject, he embraces.
     He pities those weak and tender;
     their redeemer—merciful, just.

May gold of Sheba be gifted;
prayers of blessing rise—be lifted!
     Bless us with fruitful composure.
May your fame endure as the sun:
light shining bright on everyone.
     Praise to God—holy cynosure;
     may his glor'ous name be lifted!

Psalm 73
Wreathed Quatrain

God is good to the one whose heart is pure,
but as for me, my foot nearly stumbled;
I grumbled at the wicked, for I wasn't sure
why they endure instead of being humbled.

Their carefree lives are taken in stride;
oversupplied, entitled, fleshy fools!
Blasphemy drools from mocking mouths, snide;
they drip with pride like a royal drips in jewels.

Am I a fool for keeping my heart chaste?
Have I placed my hope in some cosmic illusion?
In confusion, I saw my sacrifice as waste
and faced a future of emptiness—seclusion.

When I sought your face, my sanity returned.
I discerned eternal death would be the fate
of reprobate miscreants who never learned,
whose feet turned from the narrow interstate.

You removed blinders from myopic eyes;
the fool's demise woke my soul from its trance.
You enhance my spirit with counsel wise.
You rise to lift me to your holy manse.

Who in heaven but my Savior will pray
and sway divine wrath away from my soul?
Make me whole; be light on that dark day
when decay comes to devour me whole.

The wicked, they will not live in your midst;
those who resist your glory will not stand.
But you planned that the righteous would subsist,
will forever exist at your right hand.

Psalm 74
Mathnawi

Remember us, O God, your forsaken sheep,
and your covenant that you once swore to keep.

Turn your toes to the land where the wicked roared,
bashing stones with hammer, and flesh with the sword.

They burned and they razed and they bashed—they effaced—
tried, in pride, to have Israel's name erased.

How long will our silent prophets remain mute
while you embrace our mockers without dispute?

Ageless God of salvation, 'twas your right hand
that broke heads of sea creatures upon the sand;

divvied up their souls and served a desert feast
by teeming shores where flowing currents once ceased.

Both sun and moon dangle on a puppet's string;
that dance over summer, fall, winter, and spring.

Foes like ravens circle overhead and caw,
mocking doves caught in ravenous, hungry jaw.

Cause all dark places to cough up the greedy;
receive praises due from the poor and needy!

Do not ignore the enemy's teeth and claws;
rise up, mighty God, and defend your just cause!

Psalm 75
Monchielle Stanza

The name of God is near—
that holy name, we praise!
At his appointed time—
he'll swallow up the Earth
and churn its chaff to chyme.

The name of God is near—
O boastful, do not boast;
haughty men, full of scorn!
Judgment belongs to God,
so do not lift your horn.

The name of God is near—
within his hand, a cup
filled with wrath from the kegs.
The lips of wicked men
shall drink it to its dregs.

The name of God is near—
the righteous shall declare!
Evil shall be sifted
from the Earth, but the pure
in heart shall be lifted.

Psalm 76
Novelinee

Name of the Lord, a sword, Israel wields;
Zion—fortress, celestial brigade.
His armory walls display dented shields,
stripped from mighty generals who he slayed.
Warriors—valiant, pose behind glass,
menagerie in museum of wax.
Sonic booms of wrath, dark sound waves that pass,
falling on deaf ears like a wielded ax.
Let all the Earth be silent—turn your backs

on sacrifice that conjured holy rage,
that filled God's nostrils with nidorous stench,
that unleashed hounds of heaven, now uncaged,
and caused Judge of all to rise from his bench.
Who of us can stand 'neath your pure fury?
When your gavel crashes down on its block,
who will stand righteous before your jury?
God will receive gifts of fear from his flock;
name of the Lord, a sword, Israel's Rock.

Psalm 77
Elegy

Audible words hit ether,
swallowed up in the veiled brume, plastering these four walls,
closing in on me like a siege of befogged soldiers
come to occupy my mind.
My soul refuses comfort,
it melts like wax 'neath the blazing brow of flickering flame,
igniting sparks dry as memories of mercies faded;
my murmuring spirit weeps.

Endless days, moonlight dismissed;
anxieties, like tent pegs, stretching weary eyelids wide.
I reminisce upon those long-forgotten lullabies—
a balm to my heart, forlorn.
Will God forever ignore,
his compassions caged like rain within storm clouds during drought?
Could his affections quicken and from grave clothes be unbound,
or is love decayed, deceased?

I will not forget your deeds!
The sight of you widened the blue oculus of the sea;
the clouds cried out in terror, releasing thunder and tears;
the earth, it trembled and shook!
Path cut through a sea of glass
with bolt of lightning wielded by lapidary unseen;
chiseling hidden footprints in barren floor of the sea,
on dry ground, I follow thee.

Psalm 78
Elder Edda

O lambs, listen
to lessons, holy,
incline thy minds
to musings, wise.
Oracles declare
dark dictums, uttered—
forgotten fables
from annals, old.

We will not hide
wise sayings, spoken;
by rote, deliver
delightful recitals
that tell of all
thy loving wonders;
your famous feats
revealed from on high.

Angel-wrestler,
witness appointed,
testimony used
to teach twelve tribes.
Instruction for
in-utero votaries
who will one day
worship the Lord.

Bypassed forefathers'
footprints in sod;
their hearts hardened,
haughty with pride.
Bellicose men
bent on rebellion;
ardor-bowers
barren, empty, dry.

The Ephraimites
endowed for battle
with both arrow
and the bow armed
could not comply
with cov'nant laws
required—refused
to regard his charge.

Despised his deeds,
designed for glory;
forgot his works—
wonders, displayed.
In land of Ham,
harvest fields of Zoan,
his own, delivered
from death and slav'ry.

He split the sea
so they could pass;
the waves stood tall
and stiff, saluting.
Cloud canopy
convoyed by day,
fiery lights
ignited empyrean.

He dug deep wells,
water spewed forth,
faucets rent from rocks,
rivers from granite.
Sinners, satisfied—
once they imbibed—
ceased to thirst for
their desert-guide's leading.

In their hard hearts,
hidden away,
temptations rose
within to test him.
They bellyached
for buffet-storm
to rain down in
deluge—drench them.

"He struck a stone,
surely he can also
manufacture
meat from heaven!"
A serpent declared,
"Can't a deity who
derricked drink from boulder
also give bread of life?"

The Lord lowered
aural-ladles
to cup complaints
from soul-cauldrons, boiling.
Its bitter broth
burned holy tongue
of sovereign-chef,
sorry he had fed them.

Still, he accessed
azure-silos;
sent a grainstorm
and gave them manna.
Sinners supped on
seraphic-grist,
insisted upon via
omniv'rous grumb'ling.

Unlocked cages, freed
funnel-cougars;
broke leashes latched
to leopard-breezes.
Rained down fresh quail—
frantic demand—
a sand-picnic
spread by sovereign hand.

War cries arose,
a venter-battalion,
eager to devour
delicious spoils.
Even as fowl-flesh
flossed teeth, greedy—
loam-giant jaws gaped,
gobbled, digested.

Exequy-survivors,
shrouded in black;
unbelief masked
'hind mourning veils.
Days disappeared—
dashed away as a
despoiler—caught
in cool midnight rays.

Sepulcher-smile—
stone teeth set in sand gums,
dune-grimace summoned
sorrow and regret.
Granite gravestones
invoked grief, softened
hearts stony; rekindled
for Rock, Most High.

They waxed eloquent
with words, insincere,
smeared falsehoods with
filthy tongues, tined.
Flattery failed to veil
vascular-voices—
a clashing choir
of cov'nant breakers.

Deity atoned—
delib'rate amnesia;
he did not return
dissenters to dust.
Can man of ashes
adore what is holy?
Can wind stand still
as a statue, frozen?

Rebellion revolved—
ran sand circles;
again and again
Adonai provoked.
He put down a path;
paved hydra-street—
a feat forgotten
before shore was reached.

The Lay of the Plagues

Before Pharaoh, he
flexed sovereign muscle,
laid him flat like crushed
flax in fields of Zoan.
He slit the Nile's throat—
it thrashed, it screamed—
its streams bled out
in blind fury.

Crops cowered beneath
vast beetle-bower,
flying in swarms o'er
fields of barley.
Leggy-lodgers
leapt into town,
a green-coterie,
croaking, devouring.

Cicada-scythes
slashed heads of grain;
durum-reapers,
decapitated.
Frozen tears fell
from cumulonimbus
eyes, cattle and
vines crushed asunder.

The Lord set loose
celestial-Cerberus—
whose untold names are
Wrath, Indignation,
and Deep Distress.
Destroying angels
blazing trails down
paths of burning anger.

Barren bosom hewn—
a hollow womb
marked with moniker
in marble, chiseled.
Infertile sod,
she sobs and weeps,
for her soil-arms,
no seed embraces.

But midnight cry
revived cold hopes
of would-be mothers'
morbid wailings.
Festive dance with Death—
firstborn-masquerade;
the grave gave birth,
but mortals miscarried.

Holy slave-herder
stole his flock from
fangs of pall-panther;
plucked them from the fire.
Led them all to
lush green pastures,
broke yokes of horror,
restored their souls.

Cerulean-tongues
tasted flesh of soldiers;
saltwater sputum
splashed chariot wheels.
Kelp-nooses clutched
toga collars, choked
Pharaoh's army—
plunged them 'neath rollers, wild.

He led them to his
holy hill, hid them
in silhouette
of Sinai's shadow.
Annihilated
nations, procured
a possession
for his peoples, chosen.

Took homeless tribes;
in tents, he tucked them;
yet they still tested
testimonies, rebelled.
They turned away
in treachery, their
thankless hearts pounded—
pining for their chains.

Ire-irons poked
pious logs of wrath;
wrought iron ingots
into idols, smelt.
Cherub-criers
conveyed reports:
"Once stoked hearts, now
smoldering flames!"

Blood siphoned out
of ossein-tent;
a cold, felt shell—
a corpse of canvas.
Marrow of mercy
moldered away;
Shiloh's aorta—
asystole.

Freedom exchanged
for captivity,
glory swapped for
sword of slav'ry.
Hot wrath outpoured
on orphans, mourning,
their only balm,
a blade's embrace.

Young men whose hearts
once heaved with zeal,
lie cauterized
in cold cadavers.
New brides' wide eyes
well with sadness:
hope pulverized
by pestle of fate.

Priests fell facedown
before steel-alter,
bowed to the blade
of blind devotion.
Black-clad widows
wandered—slithered;
a piceous-serpent
striping golden sand.

The Lord awoke—
a madman besot
by libations—
lashing at men
made of thin air.
His enemies
exiled to shame-prisons
in perpetuum.

Turned up his nose
at nomens—both
Ephraim and Joseph,
chose Judah to
charter his fame.
Fixed his eyes on
Zion—his bride,
his beloved, his flame.

Temple rafters
reached the heavens,
solid groundwork
girded to earth.
Set up a throne
and sat upon it,
a shepherd-king
from sheepfolds, stolen.

From the pasture
to the palace,
royal-herdsman,
he preserved them.
With rod and staff,
with strong right arm,
with upright heart
he upheld them.

Psalm 79
Blank Verse

Wind
Bandits blow like a derecho
into your holy house.
Hear their howling in the spinning winds
like grinning whirlwolves baying?
Preying on your servants' fears, they
pierce with spears and blast
from bow echoes, sharp arrows.
Vultures peck at morsels, mortal,
laid out amongst the ruins
where blood is lapped by hounds, feral.
Rivals stroll down ghost-town streets,
stumbling over crumbling heaps of
carnal bricks and cinder bones.

Fire
Sovereign breath bellows,
igniting jealous flames;
searing birth pains seize tombs of flesh:
"How long, O Lord must we labor in vain?"
Conceive mercy; deliver us from shame!
Extinguish your burning wrath;
cauterize kingdoms that
despise your name.
Slay the wyvern, in whose grip
our souls are cowering,
douse his nostrils' blaze,
file down jagged teeth, devouring.

Earth
Rock eternal, do not let your mind range
or drift or be swift to find fault.
Bedrock vaults inhume quaking hearts,
sounding off iniquitous temblor.
Your tender mercies, white,
entrain an avalanche
of salvation—pure and fierce—
delivering bairns from dead hangs by
dynos of grace.
Place cairns upon the summit,
bearing your great name.
Rock of my salvation—erupt!
Atoning lava flow!
Bring boastful moguls to their knees—
make your presence known!

Water
Captain of my soul! My gurgling spirit plunges,
lunges 'neath rollers of wrath, submerged!
Souse my soul in power—preserve my life,
doomed to lie on floor of briny deep.
Return like the tide to tie taunting tongues,
lapping shores of mercy, cringing,
spitting out. Cringing, spitting out...
Lead your sheep by waters still,
wade with us in crimson currents
'til our hearts ebb and flow with love
toward our source.
Force the dams to break; floodwaters, raise!
Make your peoples a surging choir—
tributaries of praise!

Psalm 80
Trijan Refrain

Good Shepherd, lead us like a flock
in folds of mercy, hem;
for you have been Manasseh's rock
and the joy of Ephraim.
Let your face shine on all depraved,
stir up your might, free those enslaved.
Let your face shine
Let your face shine
Good Shepherd, may your sheep be saved!

O Lord God of hosts, O how long
must we eat bread of tears,
or listen to our rival's songs,
their mockery and jeers?
Restore us, God, O hear our prayer;
forget your anger and repair.
Restore us, God
Restore us, God
O Lord God of hosts, your wrath spare!

Deliverer, you brought a vine,
plucked out of Egypt's sand;
and it, by your sovereign design,
took root and filled the land.
The walls crumble and our foes reach,
to steal your fruit through broken pleach.
The walls crumble
The walls crumble
Deliverer, repair the breach!

O God of hosts, look down and see
your precious vine, dying,
trampled down by the enemy,
your crushed grapes all crying:
"Give ear, O God, listen—incline;
turn our tears, bitter, into wine!"
Give ear, O God
Give ear, O God
O God of hosts let your face shine!

Psalm 81
Zenith

Sing for joy to God our might,
to the God of Jacob, sing aloud,
play the harp and the tambourine,
begin the music for God's delight.
Sound the ram's horn that all the crowd
may feast 'neath new moon—pale, serene.
This is an ordinance, a statute decreed,
established in Egypt when we left in distress,
and we heard an unknown voice
declare from the thundercloud we had been freed
from the burdens, the work, the stress.
And now, O Israel, here is your choice:
follow the Lord all the days of your life,
then your mouth will be filled with honey and wheat,
your foes will all depart;
but if you insist on living in strife *too often*
and following your own conceit, *I do.*
the Lord will resign you to your stubborn heart.

Psalm 82
Sestet

The "gods" assemble at his throne,
where all their evil is made known.
Defend the needy, poor, and weak
from wicked ones whose lives they seek.
Destroy the "gods" who have no worth;
rise up, O God, and judge the Earth.

Psalm 83
Rondine

The Earth silent—omnipotence muted.
Temple shaken, a fifth column rises;
crumbling rock comminates sacred mises.
Storehouses ransacked—treasured ones looted.
Turn sentences unjustly commuted!
Midion mulch!—Endor fertilizes
all of the Earth.

They ground down pastures into coarse stover.
File down to dust, abrade them to ashes!
Bury them 'neath peals of thund'rous laughter
'til they bow down to the Master over
all of the Earth!

Psalm 84
Rosemary

How lovely is your dwelling place, O Lord.
My heart, my soul cries out, you are adored...
A place near your altar, O Lord, my King!
> Blessed are the ones who ever praise you,
> blessed are the ones whose strength you renew,
they pass through the valley, a place of springs,
from strength to strength 'til their Savior they meet.
> O Lord, hear my prayer, your ear to me yield,
> O God, look with favor upon our shield.
May I dwell in your courts, bow at your feet.
You give honor, O Lord, my shield, my sun,
you bless the faithful when their lives are done.

Psalm 85
Cyhydedd hir

God, call a ceasefire
Pull us from the mire
Set aside your ire
Restore again!
Thwart wrath assailing
Pity our wailing
Your love unfailing;
our salvation!

Heart: love what is right
Land: mercy, invite
Love and Peace: unite
in wedded bliss!
Faithfulness geyses
Harvest sun rises
The Lord, he prizes
our righteousness!

Psalm 86
Half Measure

Bend thy ear, sympathize
with my dirt-poor estate.
My heart rent, cauterize,
for I hail your name great.

My sins they numerate,
pave steps to Abaddon.
My dry soul, saturate
with spirits that gladden.

You, O Lord, will forget
all my sins committed,
for your grace will offset
my crimes, now acquitted.

Your name alone be praised,
none other do I know;
all nations fall, amazed,
their knees bent like a bow.

You do great, wondrous deeds,
for you are God alone,
and from your mouth proceeds
wisdom to man, unknown.

Teach me your verity,
that I might fear your name,
walk in integrity—
worship with soul aflame!

Ruthless men seek my end,
your name, they do not dread,
but your love doth ascend
the abode of the dead.

Though you are slow to wrath,
in due time, you will place
all my foes on a path
that leads to their disgrace.

Psalm 87
Dickson Nocturne

Mercy and love conflate—
mortar of Zion's gate—
upon the hill.
Everywhere far and wide—
piercing the great divide—
a Savior crucified
upon the hill.
Book of Life—in the vaults—
opens up and exalts
the saints who will
join dancers as they waltz
upon the hill.

Psalm 88
Luc Bat

Never-ceasing anguish;
pain and sorrow languish. My soul
shrieks loudly, and my whole
life draws near to Sheol. The dead
are my allies. My bed
is made of darkness. Dread covers
me like a shroud—hovers
like jealousy when lovers spar.

Your wrath, it burns to char,
leaving a grotesque scar behind.
I can no longer find
friends whose hearts once entwined as one,
who once loved, but now shun—
they turn around and run in fear.

Every day, I draw near
and pray that you will hear my cries.
But once a sinner dies,
can one departed rise to praise
like in his former days?
Can deaf ears hear the phrase: "I save;
I raise life from the grave!"
And can mere darkness stave what's bright,
or the grip of death smite
his will? In morning light I cry,
"Lord, do not let me die!
Do not let my soul fly away!
Do not hide when I pray!"

From my very first day, the pale
rider's hooves did assail,
melting armor and mail to dross,
attempting to emboss
an emblem of my loss and shame.

Not even Death can tame
your wrath once its hot flame ignites!
Once the tempest incites
wild waters and excites the sea
with waves surrounding me.
You caused my friends to flee, to leave;
my soul, left to bereave,
but will gladly receive—anguish.

Psalm 89
English Quintain

Your steadfast love, it makes me sing;
my mouth makes known your devotion.
Your faithfulness, your cov'nanting,
your throne, your own name's promotion,
your steadfast love, as boundless as the ocean.

Let all the heavens praise your deeds,
for who is like you in the skies?
Who among heav'nly beings exceed
the name all nature glorifies?
Lord of hosts, your throne is feared, is awesome—prized.

You rule the raging of the sea,
baptize Rahab with surging arm.
Tabor and Hermon fearlessly
sail through Sirens' silent alarm;
lulled by the melody of their Savior's charms.

Justice, the footstool of your throne;
ardent love, faithfulness, its head.
Bless the festal shout of your own,
who down dark paths of light are led,
who refuse to rest 'til God is exulted!

You are our strength, our glory, horn,
holy one of Israel, our shield!
Vision given to ancient born—
chosen king, covenant revealed;
a royal balm anoints; a wounded race, healed.

My servant, David, he shall stand
'neath battering ram of the foe.
On the sea, I will set his hand,
his right hand on rivers that flow,
crying out, "No other Father do I know!"

I will call forth his firstborn heir;
set him above all other thrones.
Keep him 'neath wing of cov'nant care,
I will protect all of his bones—
will make his offspring a wall of mighty stones.

If his children forget, forsake,
or violate the Lord's commands,
my rod shall beat, my heart shall break,
but my unfailing love withstands;
I myself will supply what my law demands.

But you have cast off, rejected;
your anointed incurs your wrath.
Crown of dust, cov'nant neglected;
breached walls fall in the aftermath;
foes expose him—a dethroned idiopath.

All who pass, they scorn, they plunder;
cheer at the ruin of his name.
Sword unforged, war, torn asunder;
sovereign quiver, arrows took aim,
cut short anointed days, covered him in shame.

How long, Lord, will you wear silence
like a cloak of fury, burning;
browbeat man with threats of violence—
molten sulfur boiling, churning?
Vanity! Vanity! Futile, our yearning!

Why have you withdrawn your favor,
your faithfulness sworn to the king?
How can you digest and savor
all their disdain and their mocking?
O Lord, save us—servants of your anointing!

Psalm 90
Muzdawidj

Our dwelling place through epochs past,
since sovereign speech sparked Big Bang's blast;
unfurling cosmic pavilion—vast.

A thousand years are but yesterday
to unfading flesh that resists decay.
While feeble man crumbles back to clay,

wiped like rheum after dark night visions,
or scion severed by scythe incisions;
stripped vines now pruned of their provisions—

secret sins exposed along the path,
illumined by omnipotent wrath—
lifeless limbs lost in the aftermath.

Seventy years we shall remain,
eighty, if strength does not wane,
but all are spent in toil and vain.

Teach us to number all our days;
to bask beneath each new morning's rays
with anthems of our heartfelt praise!

Blot out all days, gloomy and gory,
write a happy ending for our story.
May all we do bring you glory!

Psalm 91
Dixdeux

Tabernacle beside the Lord Most High;
cry aloud his name—abide in his bright
     shadow.
At sorrows, scoff—laugh loud at disaster;
the fowler's fangs cannot fathom his fierce
     pinions.
The terrors of night shall be a lullaby;
arrows—shot from strings of harps and weeping
     cellos,
shall pierce through mail—their haunting melodies
shall maul en masse and topple over ten
     thousand.
Fear not! This army of arpeggios
shall tiptoe past your tents, saluting in
     rev'rence.
Angel wings, like lute strings, plucking up—down,
prancing on adder heads—lion's teeth, tap
     dancing!
The Lord has attuned his ears to my pain,
in love, he hears, and when I cry, he will
     answer.

Psalm 92
Empat Empat

Let us give thanks to the Lord, the Most High;
raise accolades to his name in the morning.
Lute and lyre, your melodies gyre to the sky—
harmonious halos, laurels adorning.

His thoughts, deep shafts, penetralia, hidden;
let us give thanks to the Lord, the Most High!
Though his foes flourish, they will mulch to midden;
they will melt away like snowflakes in July.

I will look on their downfall with my own eyes;
my ears will hear their wretched wailings of doom.
Let us give thanks to the Lord, the Most High;
who anoints his faithful with fragrant perfume.

They bloom like cedars, butterfly-kissing clouds;
bearing fruit, lifting branches up to the sky.
Shout of his righteousness, shout it out aloud!
Let us give thanks to the Lord, the Most High!

Psalm 93
Fletcher

The Lord is robed in majesty and pow'r,
      glory extreme,
armed with strength, he rules from heaven's tower,
      reigning supreme.
The world established firmly can't be moved;
his throne, sublime,
      his power proved,
      his statutes firm, shall stand through endless time.

The sea has lifted its voice in glory,
      mighty its waves;
breakers thunder out their awesome story;
      holy octaves
are sung by pounding choirs lifting notes high
      his majesty
      from shore to sky;
the Lord shall reign through all eternity.

Psalm 94
Enclosed Triplet

God of blazing vengeance, shine and rise;
rise up from your stall and judge proud dust.
Doest please you to look upon haughty eyes,

while "Aye!s" of corrupt juries damn the just?
Just how long shall the wicked afflict the wise,
our "Why?s" and "How Long!s" muffled 'neath disgust?

They discussed your strength, said, "He does not reign!"
Rein in the reapers, tear up the tares
whose terrors deceive, kill, destroy, and feign

your fane on Salem's hill—house of your heirs!
Errors of the wicked pound down like a rain;
arraign these foolish eyes and ears of theirs.

There's one exalted above all the rest;
wrest sin from his heart and make him whole
as hole is dug for wicked without inquest.

In quest for justice, don't forget my soul!
My sole desire is that you won't, in jest,
ingest iniquity—blot me from your roll!

Roll over the wicked, O God, take a stand!
Stand in the gap for my life—my foot slips;
slip your arm 'round me, I need your right hand!

Hand the wicked justice, loosen evil's grip;
grip your foes with fear, banish them from your land,
land them in the pit, their memory, eclipse.

Psalm 95

Sonnetina Cinque

Sing to the Lord with joyful sound,
for no other king could be found
in all the Earth, in all the sea;
no god as great or as mighty.
O, come and worship him, bow down!

Hardened hearts, why do you protest;
why withhold that which should be confessed?
Forty years, you wandered astray,
in blindness, could not see the way,
took path of wrath and saw no rest.

Psalm 96
Kyrielle

Sing to the Lord a song that's new,
sing to the Lord the praise he's due;
sing to the Lord, proclaim his fame,
sing to the Lord and praise his name.

He made the heavens and the Earth,
he's clothed in splendor, strength, and worth;
all of their "gods" need hide in shame;
sing to the Lord and praise his name.

We tremble at his holiness,
we bring our off'rings, we confess
and ask him to forgive our blame;
sing to the Lord and praise his name.

The Lord will judge, O, Earth, rejoice;
all that he made, sing with one voice;
in righteousness the world reclaim;
sing to the Lord and praise his name.

Psalm 97
Douzet

The distant shores rejoice, the Lord God reigns.
His justice, the foundation of his throne.
His foes on ev'ry side are overthrown;
his lightning lights the world, his word ordains.

The mountains melt like wax before the Lord;
the people see his glory, hear his fame,
those who boast in idols are put to shame,
while Zion shouts for joy with one accord.

The Lord Most High all other gods disdains.
He guards the lives of those he calls his own.
His light upon the upright heart outpoured.
You righteous, shout for joy and praise his name!

Psalm 98
Dr. Seuss

O sing to the Lord,
a new song never sung;
let words of his works
trip off of your tongue.

Marvelous miracles,
phenomenal feats
when his reverent right hand
and his holy arm meets!
He reveals righteousness to every nation,
makes known his power and his salvation!

Memory clapper swings; steadfast love rings a bell;
tolling—peals rolling—inside the ears of Israel.
Eyeballs of the Earth all beholding, all peeking;
the salvation of their God, searching for—seeking.

Cheerful noise makers,
churn out noises cheerful;
break forth into song,
give the whole world an earful!

Peppy poems, perky praises—
blue, welkin-roof our song raises!

Lute, harp and lyre,
brassy blan bloppers;
trumpets and horns,
flashy flan floppers,
make a joyful noise—
Bop! Boom! Bang! Bing!
Blast out a ditty
to our great God and King!

O the sounds that we will make—we will shake, shout, and sing!

Let the sea roar—
a giant blue lion;
a surging wave offering
rolling toward Zion.

Let the hills leap
when the rivers cause
them to dance to the rhythm
of their thund'rous applause!

The Father's footsteps falling, descending—drumming—
swift sounds of our just judge's imminent coming;
for all those who are left, he will make all things right,
judging with equity all peoples within his sights.

O the sounds that we will make—we will shake, shout, and sing!

Psalm 99
Standard Habbie

This heart of mine, it leaps and swings,
chasing the trail of wand curlings—
a baton held in angel's wings,
conducting a choir
made up of blood-bought queens and kings,
Christ's blood spilled to sire.

Spread his glory and spread his fame!
Let all of the peoples proclaim,
"Holy and just, his awesome name;
justice, our God shall mete!"
Hearts his holiness set aflame,
come worship at his feet!

He answers prayers of sinful men;
within the cloud, he spoke to them—
affirmed his statutes once again
and promised to forgive.
All sinful acts he shall condemn,
but sinful man shall live!

Psalm 100
Baccreseize

Rejoice in Him

Give thanks to God, give thanks to God,
cry out his praise, give thanks to God.
The hearts of those who seek the Lord—
      Rejoice in Him.
Look to the Lord, rejoice in him,
make known to all what he has done,
give thanks to God, give thanks to God—
      Rejoice in Him.
Sing praise to him for all his works,
look to the Lord and to his strength,
let all who seek his face with joy—
      Rejoice in Him.

Psalm 101
Strambotto Romagnuolo

A plainsong rises, chanting steadfast love
to the rhythm of your justice, booming like a drum.
O Lord, when will you descend from above
and lead me to the city from which the blameless come?
As for me and my house, we shall serve the Lord,
refusing to bow down to what paupers can afford.
On a banquet of evil I will not feast;
I will reject the sin that clings like fleas to a beast.

I shall silence lips that slip and slander
and will forsake all sinners sinister and gloomy,
favor footfalls of friends that don't meander,
and I will bless the blameless who minister to me.
I shall shut out all those who cause division,
wipe out connivers like woeful tears blurring vision.
With holy harrow, I will till the land,
uprooting evildoers with my righteous right hand.

Psalm 102
Byr a Thoddaid

Lord, my God, will you please listen
to the cry of my petition?
Hide not your visage behind a shadow!
Know my deep distress—bind

aural cords to my soul's longing;
command grace to cease prolonging!
My days they pass like a smokestack ablaze—
they raze, they burn, they stoke.

In scorching heat, my dead heart fades,
it shrivels like worn, trodden blades.
My empty belly is so thin it groans;
my bones cling to my skin.

Memories recur and haunt me;
enemies, they mock and taunt me.
Under the weight of your frown and deep wrath
I hath been crushed—thrown down.

You, O Lord, throughout the ages
have not paid Zion's sins her wages.
You have shown from above, patient pity,
your city saved by love.

Let this one truth be recorded—
o'er all peoples God hath lorded.
He looked down in sympathy; where death loomed,
those doomed souls, he set free!

In my youth, my strength was broken;
my dead heart revived—awoken!
You laid the foundation—land and the sea—
artistry of your hand!

You shall slay all wicked varmints—
wear them out like tattered garments.
Immutable Father, he will never
sever his ties with me.

Psalm 103
Lyric

Bless the Lord, O my soul,
with all that is within;
forget not all his benefits and
he shall forget your sin.
He cures all of your sickness;
from the pit, he restores.
He sets your strength on eagle's wings;
it rises and it soars!

Justice is worked for the oppressed;
God makes known his ways.
The Lord is merciful and kind;
his hand of wrath, he stays.
Yahweh abounds in steadfast love;
he will not always chide;
his anger fades, it does not last;
he casts our sins aside.

The space between the earth and sky—
all below and above.
So is the measure of his grace—
and the breadth of his love.
The Lord, our Father, shows compassion
on all who fear and trust;
for he remembers our weakness—
that we were formed from dust.

As for man, his days are grass,
fast fading like the flowers;
when a strong wind o'er wilted petals pass,
it crushes and devours.
But the Lord, his steadfast love,
from age to age remains
on those who keep his covenant
and from all sin refrain.

The Lord has established his throne;
he rules over all;
bless the Lord, all you, his angels,
who heed his voice and call.
Bless the Lord, you heavenly host,
ministers who extol
his dominion over all things.
Bless the Lord, O my soul.

Psalm 104
Dr. Stella

The Lord is clothed with majesty,
in light—holy raiment;
he makes the clouds his chariot,
and rides on wind-swept wings.
The Earth, set by his sole decree,
flees at his voice—clamant;
snags moguls with his lariat;
they bow, kiss signet rings.

Springs gush forth, fill barren valleys,
hydrate all God's creatures;
serenaded by chirping birds,
from treetop perches—trill.
Parched hills drink tears from clouded eyes—
witnesses in bleachers—
looking down upon plants and herds,
marveling at God's skill.

Till the earth, bring forth food and wine,
that heart of man gladdens.
Raise cedars like a maestro's wand,
conducting birds that sing.
The moon, it marks the seasons—shines;
darkness marks Abaddon.
When light of day, like cloak, is donned,
man labors 'til evening.

In wisdom, you have made all things,
ocean depths, abyssal,
brimming with creatures great and small,
teeming below swift ships.
You hide your face; despair, it clings—
withdrawn grace—dismissal.
Deep watery grave, sodden pall,
death grips—submerged soul slips.

O God, may your glory endure—
rejoice in your splendor!
The Earth it trembles and it smokes,
in rev'rence sing—extol!
I will give praise to your name, pure—
meditation, tender;
but sinners, their grace he revokes;
bless the Lord, O my soul!

Psalm 105
Wordsworth Sestet

Call upon the name of the Lord, shout praise;
among the peoples, let his deeds be known.
Sing! Sing! Sing of wond'rous works he has shown,
revealed in hearts that seek him and rejoice;
songs of his strength and his miracles—raise,
servants, offspring, children of sovereign choice.

He is our God; his judgments fill the Earth.
He will forget his promises never;
twenty thousand years, they could not sever
covenant cords that bind us to oaths, sworn.
When his people were few—of little worth—
his anointed, saved from oppression—scorn.

He summoned a famine, broke off their bread,
but sent ahead a man sold as a slave;
a boy in bondage, a tethered thrall—knave—
bound by unfulfilled prophecies spoken,
until the king lifted shame from his head;
freed from fetters and iron chains, broken.

Israel sojourned in the land of Ham,
where they prospered and bore fruit of power;
jaws of their foes, bore fangs to devour,
but the Lord sent servants to deliver.
The land went to war with the great I AM;
ten plagues shot from omnipotent quiver.

Darkness fell, land shadowed by a black shroud;
the waters turned red as a shame-faced thief,
the land swarmed with frogs, causing woe and grief.
Gnats invaded, the land flooded with flies;
hail fell, the crops and livestock struck down—bowed—
wrath unappeased 'til every firstborn dies!

Israel fled on wings of silver—gold,
'neath cloud of fire—their light, their covering;
food fell from heaven, spirit hovering,
thirst quenched by water gushing from a Rock.
He remembered his promise, oath foretold;
with singing and joy, he rescued his flock.

Psalm 106
Rubaiyat

Give thanks to the Lord, his love, enduring;
his mighty deeds, praiseworthy—alluring!
All who observe justice, they shall be blessed;
at rest in righteousness, reassuring.

Remember me, Lord, this is my request:
save me from guilt exposed by your inquest
that I may rejoice in gladness, holy—
robes of your inheritance, finely dressed.

Both we and our fathers have sinned wholly;
failed to praise your wondrous works solely.
But rebelled by the shore of the Red Sea,
where your might made us bow, meek and lowly.

For your own name's sake, you set captives free,
paved path of escape from their enemy.
Brought them out safely, set them on the shore
while waters deluged the adversary.

But they remembered his goodness no more
as soon as their sandals hit desert floor.
Their wanton cravings angered God, tested,
tempting him to renege all that he swore.

Men of the camp rose up, rebelled, wrested
power from Moses and Aaron, blessed;
terra jaws unhinged, swallowed rebel priests;
fire consumed, deep loam venter digested.

In Horeb, true worship for the Lord ceased;
swapped his glory for images of beasts.
They forgot their Savior—all of his deeds—
Moses—chosen one—stood in the gap breached.

Standing with his staff, he prays—intercedes,
to stave off wrath their idolatry feeds.
They despised the garden, tilled up ruction,
pulled up plants flowering from promise seeds.

In tents, they murmured—ignored instruction—
followed hearts down dark paths of seduction;
offspring fell, scattered among the nation,
provoked raised right arm to wreak destruction.

They looked to Baal for their consecration,
trusting in gods with no animation;
but Phinehas rose, and the plague was stayed—
righteousness praised through all generations.

At Meribah waters, they disobeyed;
Moses spoke rashly; commandments, betrayed.
Their enemies lingered, became a snare;
God's favor departed; rebellion raved.

Idols embraced them, they became ensnared;
their children dragged down into a nightmare.
Their land was polluted, Canaan, blood-soaked;
their hard hearts petrified into despair.

The wrath of the Lord was ignited—stoked—
sin of his people, incited—provoked;
their enemies invaded and oppressed;
ten thousand times were his mercies evoked!

He looked upon them—helpless, distressed—
remembered his covenant, acquiesced.
Because of his pity, because of care,
by the hand of their captors, they were blessed.

Save us, O God, from our enemies' snare,
that we may shout praise to One just and fair,
"Blessed be your name forever and ever!"
May, "Amen! Praise the Lord!" be our prayer!

Psalm 107
Blues Stanza

Give thanks to the Lord, shout praise from your mouth,
let thanksgiving flow from out of the mouth,
of rivers winding east, west, north and south.

They wandered through wastelands—desert holes,
they cried to the Lord—hearts riddled with holes,
he delivered them, satisfied their souls.

Some sat in darkness—the shadow of death,
they cried to God, "Deliver us from death!"
Give thanks for his love until dying breath.

Some were fools who wandered through sinful ways;
he saved those near death, those who lost their ways.
Tell of his deeds in thankful songs of praise!

Some went down in ships, in great waters deep;
courage sank into pits, in darkness deep,
but he drew them out, their souls he did keep.

He turns dry desert into thirsty ground,
turns grapes of wrath into sweet wine he's ground.
Blessings are multiplied, the lost are found.

On evil princes, his contempt is poured,
but on the needy, his grace is outpoured.
Consider the steadfast love of the Lord!

Psalm 108
Decathlon

My heart is steadfast, O my God,
with all my soul I sing to you.
      O harp, awake!
O dawn, I will awaken you
      with songs aloud;
may nations hear my songs of praise,
of faithfulness through endless days
      that none can shake.
Exalted are you, God, above the skies,
and let your glory o'er the Earth arise.

O save us, God, with your right hand,
deliver those you love, O Lord;
      God hears, he speaks:
"In triumph I will judge your foes
      and seize the land
for Gilead is mine to hold
while Judah is my scepter, bold;
      Moab, the bleak,
I wash my hands of you, and toss my shoe
at Edom, while Philistia, I hew."

You have rejected us, O God,
our armies go no more to war.
      Who will lead me
to Edom, city fortified?
      O spare your rod
and give us aid against our foe.
The help of man is scant and slow,
      but God will free,
and it is he who gains the victories
and tramples in the dust our enemies.

Psalm 109
Stave Stanza

O God, awake from your slumber!
Armies of slack tongues lumber—
laps down my heart with vocal cords;
spit on my love, wave verbal swords.
Accusations, it slavers, falls,
O God, answer me when I call!

Stand false witness to my foe's right,
strike prayers from his record—indict!
Stand an accuser to his left,
his home and livelihood bereft!
May the hopes of his kindred fall;
O God, answer me when I call!

Seize all he owns to pay his debt;
his seed, disowned—feed on regret!
Prune his name from his family tree,
leave a stump of iniquity,
allow his legacy to fall.
O God, answer me when I call!

Humble hearts, he stripped of blessing,
to don curses as their dressing.
May shame soak into his bones and sipe,
soiling every last prison stripe!
Cause all who speak evil to fall;
O God, answer me when I call!

Lord, speed deliverance—quicken,
resuscitate my heart, stricken!
Night devours the shadow cast
by frame gaunt from incessant fast.
When foes look on me, gazes fall;
O God, answer me when I call!

Your steadfast love is my grapnel,
but to the wicked—sharp shrapnel
stuck in their flesh, infecting shame.
As for me, I shall praise your name;
your right arm saved me from the Fall.
O God, answer me when I call!

Psalm 110
Dizain

My LORD said, "Lord, come sit at my right hand,
your foes, a stool, at your feet, I shall make!"
O, staff of Judah, raised throughout the land,
rule amongst those who falter and forsake.
Uphold an army the earth cannot shake!
The LORD has sworn and will not change his mind:
a prince—a priest—of everlasting kind—
in wrath, this Lord shall execute your kings.
Gardens lost, but open graves you shall find,
while the victor drinks from eternal springs.

Psalm 111
Quintilla

Alleluia! Praise Adonai!
Beating heart, pay homage, pulsate;
cardio-council, congregate.
Delight! His deeds done, glorify;
Exult! Wond'rous works, magnify!

For those who fear him, he gives food;
graciously gives them provision.
His covenant, no rescission!
Inheritance for nations wooed—
just, faithful ones, he will include.

Knit together works with his hands;
laws and precepts trustworthy, true;
minted maxims, he can't eschew!
No condemnation, reprimands,
or insignia scorched by brands.

Purchased our souls, with blood, redeemed;
quenched the grave's parched thirst forever.
Rent in twain, temple veil, sever;
sov'reign hand smote what serpent schemed.
The Lord's name be ever esteemed!

Psalm 112
Envelope Stanza

Praise to the Lord! Hallelu Yah!
The man who fears the Lord is blessed;
light dawns within the darkest test
for he whose joy is in his law.

God will come, and to whom he gives;
he has no fear of tragic news;
his heart is calm, all fears refuse;
the wicked, such a man outlives.

Psalm 113
Ghazal

O servants of the Lord,
praise the name of the Lord!

From this time forth 'til endless age of ages;
bright orb raise your right arm, solar, in praise of the Lord!

Higher than nations, skies, or rich men's wages;
behold the chair in empyreal air—throne of the Lord!

Prisoners of dust, he unlocks their cages;
from the ash heap, he finds his sheep—meek lambs of the Lord!

He sets the needy among kings and sages;
rewards their toil with titles, royal—princes of the Lord!

To foul-ending fables, he adds more pages;
the arid womb will blossom, bloom, bearing heirs of the Lord!

O servants of the Lord,
praise the name of the Lord!

Psalm 114
Sweetbriar

When Judah left
Egypt behind
to be God's chosen one,
the Red Sea fled,
the mountains skipped,
the hills, like lambs, did run.

O, tremble, Earth,
the Lord is here,
his feats have just begun;
he turns the rock
into a pool;
who can compare? There's none.

Psalm 115
Boutonniere

Not to us, Lord, not to us,
glory to your faithfulness.
Nations sneer, "Where is your God?"
While to idols, mute they nod—
having eyes, they only gawk,
having mouths, they cannot talk,
having legs, they cannot walk—
statues made of gold and sod.
Trust in God, our help, our shield,
he who blesses those who yield,
hearts in him forever sealed.
Not to us, Lord, not to us,
glory to your faithfulness.

Psalm 116
Duni

Sorrow and trouble strangled my soul,
the cords of death compressed;
overcome by anguish of the grave,
affliction wrenched its toll;
dismay made me its slave.
I cried to God who heard and blessed;
he heard me and made me whole.

How can I thank him, what can I say
for all he's done for me?
Standing in the presence of his saints,
my vows to him I pay.
My thanks without restraint;
he broke my chains, he set me free,
with what can my heart repay?

Psalm 117
Etheree

Praise
the Lord
you nations;
all you peoples,
extol his great name!
Great are his affections,
and great is his love for us.
The faithfulness of the Lord God
will endure throughout all the ages.
Praise the Lord! Hallelujah! Praise the Lord!

Psalm 118
Laurel

Give thanks to the Lord—he is good;
      his steadfast love prevails.
Set free from jowls of distress—
to fear I shall not acquiesce;
when my foes attempt to oppress—
      my helper's arm avails!

As if mere man or princes could
      offer security.
Nations roared, the whole hoard rumbled,
thorns in fire, they snapped and bumbled;
I was pushed hard, almost stumbled,
      but God, he rescued me.

O Lord, my strength! O Lord, my song!
      How great is your right hand!
I will not die, my flesh won't fade
for a cornerstone has been laid—
gold stone of heaven's colonnade—
      before whom we shall stand!

"Grant us success—save—make us strong!"
      all Israel shouts and hails.
Bind festal bull to the altar,
shout praise to God from the Psalter;
his light shines, we cannot falter!
      His steadfast love prevails!

Psalm 119
22 Complete Couplets

Aleph
The Lord established precepts to obey;
blessed are the righteous who walk in his way.

Beth
How can a person walk in purity?
By living in the light of his decree.

Gimel
Reveal to me the truths hid in your law
and open up my eyes, fill me with awe.

Daleth
Keep me from wayward ways when I am lured
and strengthen me according to your Word.

He
Direct me in the path of your commands,
turn my eyes away from worthless plans.

Waw
My hope is in your law; it sets me free
to answer those who taunt me endlessly.

Zayin
My comfort is this: when the wicked are strong,
your decrees are the theme of my lifelong song.

Heth
With all of my heart, I have sought your face;
according to your promise, grant me grace.

Teth

More precious by far than silver or gold
is the law from your mouth, its wealth untold.

Yodh

I know, O Lord, that your precepts are right,
your love is my comfort, your law my delight. *may it be.*

Kaph

I look for your promise; how long must I wait
while my foes seek to annihilate?

Lamedh

Your word is eternal, your laws are pure,
all things recede, but your statutes endure.

Mem

Your law gives me insight, your precepts are sweet;
like honey in the mouth, your words I eat.

Nun

Your word is a lamp and a light to my feet.
I will keep your decrees 'til life is complete.

Samekh

I love your law; you're my refuge and shield.
I will keep your commands, my life I yield.

Ayin

Your precepts are right, so I hate ev'ry wrong;
rise up, O Lord, and show yourself strong.

Pe
Unfold your words, to the simple give light;
your statutes are wonderful, glorious, bright.

Tsadhe
When troubles assail me, your law is my joy,
enduring forever, no foe can destroy.

Qoph
I rise before dawn and cry to the Lord,
my hope is in him, in the strength of his word.

Resh
Your words, Lord, are righteous, eternal and true;
though foes persecute me, I'll not turn from you.

Sin & Shin
When rulers pursue me without any cause,
you give great peace to those who love your laws.

Taw
I long for your salvation all of my days;
may my mouth sing of your word in endless praise.

Psalm 120
Neville

I cried out in deep dejection
while shrewd slashers who speak
with sharp tongues in their cheeks,
shoot sharp arrows of rejection.
Warlords sit in their tents—
insolent malcontents—
plotting war and insurrection.

Psalm 121
Metric Pyramid

My eyes
rise to the heights,
for my helper delights—
attends, day and night, to my cries;
unmoved, I rest in the shade he supplies.
He will not slumber, he will not sleep; the moonlight's
glow, by night, will not strike, nor the sunbeams by day ignite;
the Lord, he watches over my life, with each new day a reprise.

Psalm 122
Wavelet

     The day that I went
      to your holy tent,
my heart with gladness overflowed!
Jerusalem, sacred city—
all love and unity bestowed!
     All tribes and all ranks,
      raise hands, give him thanks,
for he set David on the throne!
Lord, allot peace, grant us pity,
love us and call us all your own.
     Cause all wars to cease;
      multiply our peace.

Psalm 123
Hymnal Measure

To the one enthroned in the skies,
I wait on you alone;
to you, O Lord, I lift my eyes;
my soul, for mercy, groans.

As a servant looks to his lord
for kindness and relief,
so Father spare us from the sword
and rescue us from grief.

Our Savior, save us from our shame,
from sin, scorn, and disease;
etch on our hearts your blessed name
and your own wrath, appease.

Psalm 124
Ae Freslighe

Yahweh—if he decided—
all man's power to deprive,
our foes would have presided—
swallowed all of us alive.

Acrid rage; hot cremation—
our soul-vessel lost, capsized;
purged white by frore lavation
beneath waves of wrath—baptized.

But we were all delivered,
escaped the snares like fowls;
when our holy caregiver
muzzled their jagged jowls!

Hard hearts he heals—penetrates,
his full glory on display;
creation, he venerates,
Israel, shout praise to Yahweh!

Psalm 125
Decuain

All of those who have the proclivity
to put their whole trust in the Lord most high
shall be like an immense acclivity,
the base of which fiercest storm cannot pry.
The mountains encircle Zion like pi;
so the Lord surrounds us with charity.
The scepter's orb scowls as an evil eye,
glaring down on the just with enmity.
The Lord casts off the wicked who belie,
but gracious to those who on grace rely.

Psalm 126
Alexandrine

Restore
Zion's treasure
back to the days of yore.
Revive our mute lips with laughter,
pleasure.

Good health
and riches, great—
like streams flowing with stealth—
return to us, remunerate
our wealth.

Destroy
Once-sturdy biers;
for when our God appears,
our gracious plowman will reap joy
from our tears.

Psalm 127
Pleiades

Galaxie

Grout and mortar, laid in vain;
Godless masons—men of clay.
Grumb'ling bellies swell with pain—
Greedy—pining for the day.
God's children, they shall erect
Gates of gold—fortress foretold—
Grave of the great architect!

Psalm 128
Than Bauk

Your name I fear;
I won't veer off
from clear paths paved.

My ache is staved
by fruit craved, my
pain waived, paunch swells.

Your spouse, she dwells;
her smile tells of
deep wells of mirth.

No gold on Earth
could be worth each
new birth she bears.

For all her heirs
who say prayers and
cast cares far out

will dance and shout,
for no doubt, peace
will sprout and bloom.

Psalm 129
Serena

> My afflictions are
> great.
Traitor at my back, assailing;
irrigator, filling furrows with my blood.
Foes with weapons; war cry, wailing;
Bows and arrows fly—none prevailing.
Ingrate! Be put to shame—backward-turned;
separate like chaff, be withered, burned!
> My afflictions are
> great.
But the blessings of the Lord are even greater.

Psalm 130
Fjorton

This abyss disgorges echoes of despair;
dismiss not, Lord, this heavy heart, bleeding, raw, and bare!
Your ears to my sorrows, attune, modulate;
for tears without number, crush asunder, while my soul waits.
A complete conspectus—sin unknown or planned—
delete them all, protect us! Or whom of your saints shall stand?
Exculpation: we do not get what we deserve!
Exultation: You are holy! Your great name alone we serve!
Our souls wait—ache for your saving power,
patrol for break of day like tired troops marching upon a tower.
Accord thy heart with hope—may it boldly posit:
"The Lord, he is our Shepherd and we, his sheep, are his cosset!
Exemption from wrath; the prisoners he sets free;
Redemption to all—sinners saved from the stains of their iniquity!"

Psalm 131
Rhopalic Verse

Heart, lowborn, continue
to remain submissive.

Eyes, desist beholding
dense mockers—derisive.

Mind, divert, occupy
thy musings—wanderings;
set upon cognitions,
great, lofty, ponderings.

Soul, silent—hypnotized,
fast asleep, reposing
in embrace, paternal,
a lovesong composing.

Hope again—revival!
O Israel, glorify!
Time marches, eternal,
O peoples, testify!

Psalm 132
Diatelle

God
retain
David's pain;
hardship endured.
His vows were not in vain
to find dwelling place for the Lord.
Robed in righteousness and joy their reward,
for David's sake, find resting place, in cov'nant pod.
On beards of David's kin, oil anoints, poured
on those who fear God; sin, abstain.
On Zion's hill God reigns;
he gives poor board.
Joy! No stain
refrains
God.

Psalm 133
Roundelay

Blessed are brothers of well repute found abiding—
not avoiding dispute by exiling love into hiding,
but shamelessly shouting, "Repressed heart, be free!"
This, the love of Christ manifest in the breast of unity.

When brothers put on love like a royal costume,
are loyal to mete affections, sweet like costly perfume
on brow of our priest singing, "Blest—worship me!"
This, the love of Christ manifest in the breast of unity.

Fresh dew falling on erupting mountains, ashen;
a flowing fountain dousing fierce flames of man's flagrant passion;
cooling stoked hearts now at rest in felicity.
This, the love of Christ manifest in the breast of unity.

Psalm 134
Star Sevlin

Come! Seek his face,
all servants of Yahweh,
who kneel by night and dance by day!
Lift up your holy hands,
bless the Lord in his holy place;
maker of sky and lands,
show us your grace!

Psalm 135
Casbairdne

Praise the Lord's name, nonpareil,
sounds raise from the carillons!
Gold streets pave his citadel;
spires wave grand gonfalons!

His right hand rules—dominates;
sea and land—his achievement.
His frown, it damns—terminates;
strikes down—bitter bereavement!

Signs and wonders—tragedies;
strength of man a vagary.
Kings become bones—effigies;
their thrones—the Lord's legacy.

His name revives—awakens;
survives eons eternal.
Vows cannot be forsaken;
endows passion, paternal.

Gold, silver, lead enemies;
blind, deaf, dumb, dead, aphonic.
White-washed tombstones—threnodies
for deities, demonic.

Cease laments of confession;
frail tents of man, aurify!
This is our sole profession—
and our one goal—glorify!

May it be.

Psalm 136
Triolet

The name of the Lord—no other name equates;
his love, resolute, perdures evermore.
Endless wonders his hand alone instigates;
the name of the Lord—no other name equates!
His understanding fills the skies—saturates
the highest heavens, Earth's vale, the ocean's floor.
The name of the Lord—no other name equates;
his love, resolute, perdures evermore.

The name of the Lord—no other name equates;
his love, resolute, perdures evermore.
Light from his sun, his moon, his stars, penetrates;
the name of the Lord—no other name equates!
He struck down the firstborn behind Egypt's gates;
but bloodstained frames of Israel, death ignored.
The name of the Lord—no other name equates;
his love, resolute, perdures evermore.

The name of the Lord—no other name equates;
his love, resolute, perdures evermore.
He speaks to the sea; every surge dissipates;
the name of the Lord—no other name equates!
He speaks again and the same wave desecrates
all of Pharaoh's chariots, his horses, his corps!
The name of the Lord—no other name equates;
his love, resolute, perdures evermore.

The name of the Lord—no other name equates;
his love, resolute, perdures evermore.
He led his people along desert interstates;
the name of the Lord—no other name equates!
He conquered kings, transferred deeds of their estates
and gave them to Israel as spoils of war.
The name of the Lord—no other name equates;
his love, resolute, perdures evermore.

The name of the Lord—no other name equates;
his love, resolute, perdures evermore.
He remembered his people when in dire straits;
the name of the Lord—no other name equates!
Treaties of captivity, the Lord negates;
preserves the lives of his children, needy and poor.
The name of the Lord—no other name equates;
his love, resolute, perdures evermore.

Psalm 137
Kloang

By Babylon's shore   we wept.
Hearts, for Zion leapt   no more.
Poplar tree limbs kept   harp strings
silent. Captors roar   while Judah sings.

Sorrows, persistent;   flames fanned
in a foreign land—   distant.
O, may my right hand   lose skill
if I'm resistant   to Salem's hill.

"Down to its bedrock,   Raze! Raze!"
With aberrant praise,   they mock.
The One who repays   is blessed;
Babylon, in stocks—   is dispossessed!

Psalm 138
ZaniLa Rhyme

I sing to you, Lord, with my whole heart;
you ran to answer my call.
I will sing your praise all of my days!
You enkindled my soul from its pall.

I genuflect beneath your steeple;
lay flat at the feet of love.
All of my days, I will sing your praise!
Your name is over all things above.

Hijack the mouths of the kings of Earth
and fill them with lauds of praise.
I will sing your praise all of my days!
Debts of the lowly, Yahweh defrays.

Though I walk down a path of darkness,
you shroud me in hidden light.
All of my days, I will sing your praise!
Your steadfast love, Lord, is my delight.

Psalm 139
Collins Sestet

O Lord, you have searched me, known me;
from your throne, discerning eyes see
when I sit down and when I rise,
all secret thoughts, hidden heart-cries;
where my feet stand or my head lays,
you, O Lord, are acquainted with all of my ways.

Omniscient One, fully aware
of my ev'ry unspoken care.
Ev'ry side, I feel your embrace—
knowledge too wonderful to trace!
My spirit soars to heights of praise;
you, O Lord, are acquainted with all of my ways.

Where shall I run? Remain unseen?
Heaven or hell or in between?
Within clouds or 'neath briny deep,
even there, your right hand shall keep!
Darkness combusts—sets ablaze;
you, O Lord, are acquainted with all of my ways.

My inward parts woven like lace
within dark, hidden hiding place.
Fear, joy, and wonder serenade
Wight-Tailor and all he has made.
My frame, ever before your gaze;
you, O Lord, are acquainted with all of my ways.

Before my eyes could even look,
you penned my days within your book.
The thoughts of God—a golden gem!
How vast the sum of all of them;
countless as fields of golden maize;
you, O Lord, are acquainted with all of my ways.

Wicked men take your name in vain;
may their lives end in toil and pain.
All those who hate you, I oppose;
I count all of them as my foes.
Inspect my heart, its deeds, appraise;
you, O Lord, are acquainted with all of my ways.

Psalm 140
Gilbert

Save me from evil plots, violent;
let wickedness be staved!
Warlords load up weapon wagons,
breathing fire—the breath of dragons—
lips of venom—depraved.
They have laid out nets, cords discreet—
hidden traps to grapple my feet.

Give ear to my pleas for mercy,
O Lord, you are my God.
Thwart the plans of the devil's corps,
shield my head in the day of war,
do not hold back your rod.
May their wicked plans be halted
lest they conquer—be exalted!

May the lies of my enemies
all come back to haunt them.
Upon their heads, dump burning coals,
cast them deep into miry holes,
hunt them down and taunt them.
I know my God will plead my case,
until I see him face-to-face.

Psalm 141
Mathlish

Have compassion, Father, hear my desperate cries;
I fall before your altar, O Lord, do not despise!

My prayers rise like incense, digested in vaporous venter;
lips and mind, stand your guard! Let no evil enter!
Heart of mine, keep watch, let all of your praise center

on the light that reveals man's plight—crumbling heart and bone;
every sin, it applauds, every deed, wicked, it condones.

Let the righteous strike like dull flint strikes wet stone. In vain.
shall despots, soon deposed, threaten me with pain.
When jaws of graves, mocking, unlock—their broken bones rent in
twain!

My eyes are fixed on you, O Lord; on you I cast my cares;
save my soul from death, for your great name alone, it hallows.
Rescue me from the dark pit, my foes, and the fowler's snares;
intercept all my enemies, hang them upon their own gallows!

Psalm 142
Rhymed Cinquain

Weep a wretched sonnet;
hear my heart pleading!
Cares press down upon it,
bruising, beating, bleeding.
My soul pleads and my deeds beg for interceding.

Snagged within hidden snares,
my tethered heart beats
against dark, barbed nightmares;
my frightened soul retreats.
"No one cares or can be spared from the judgment seat!"

"O Lord, my refuge be!"
Swallowed deep in earth—
those who persecute me
intern my soul in mirth.
"Deliver me from dearth, my God of matchless worth!"

Psalm 143
Virelet

Your ears, O Lord—a stethoscope;
      my heart, auscultate!
Look past my sin and loss of hope,
      help me to bear this weight!

My enemy, he lies in wait
      to crush my soul to mote.
The darkness comes to lull—sedate—
      to ruin and to gloat.

My memories revolve in rote;
      I try to understand.
My soul dehydrates—a parched throat,
      thirsting in a barren land.

My failing spirit cannot stand;
      show me your hidden face!
May the limits of your love expand
      to lengths I cannot trace!

Deliver me, O Lord, abase
      both enemy and foe.
Instruct me your will to embrace,
      and your spirit, bestow.

Preserve my life from dole and woe,
      and rogues who interlope.
May your steadfast love for my soul grow—
      bloom into bulbs of hope.

Psalm 144
Poulter's Measure

Sergeant major of the heavens, stronghold and shield,
strengthen my feeble hands that weapons of war I may wield!
O Lord, what is man but a fleeting, shallow breath,
passing like shadows from transitory lives to their deaths?

Bear down upon the mountains 'til they tremble—slip;
cause your presence to spill over the top of heaven's lip.
Send forth your lightning—golden arrows 'cross the sky,
stretched out on bows of thunder shot from cloudy thrones on high.

Free my neck from the grip of aqueous fingers,
scrape fables from unctuous tongues where wicked slander lingers.
Upon the charango, I strum an unknown chord,
songs for our holy Champion who saves us from the sword.

May our sons rise like cedars praising deity;
daughters, caryatids, raising a palace canopy.
May our silos overflow, livestock fill the stalls;
blessed are all of God's people on whom all these blessings fall!

Psalm 145
Saraband

Extol ipseity divine;
unsearchable is his greatness!
The brightness of his good works shine
throughout every generation.
On majesty, I meditate,
his great deeds, my veneration.
Gracious Lord, when I contemplate

your love, slow to show displeasure,
glory vast, beyond all measure—
what is man that we're your treasure?
The Lord satisfies those bowed down,
who see a smile beneath his frown.
Convokes tongues for his hallowed choir,
condemns the wicked to the fire.

Psalm 146
Briolette

The soul and flesh weave and entwine;
heart and death, embrace and flatline.
Spirit within, awake! Consign
thy resolve to praise our great king—
with heart, with soul, with everything!

Do not trust czar, prince, or emir,
refuse to worship, bow, revere,
for their powers fade—disappear.
Their plans perish—final good-bye;
their last breath: a rattle, a sigh.

Blessed are those who put their trust
in a ruler both strong and just.
Who, out of nothing—out of dust—
made the heavens, the Earth, the sea,
and keeps faith for eternity.

He loves those who this world disdains;
he satisfies their hunger pains;
he sets prisoners free—breaks their chains.
To the blind, he restores vision;
to the pure, he grants provision;

To all those crushed 'neath verbal strafe;
to every widow, every waif—
he watches over, keeps them safe.
Praise the Lord! Praise Judah's lion!
Our Lord, he reigns over Zion!

Psalm 147
Ballad Stanza

Praise the Lord!

How pleasant and fitting is praise;
what joy his glory riles!
The Lord builds up Jerusalem—
gathers her lost exiles.

Great Physician heals broken hearts;
starlight strokes souls, aching.
He threads the tails of shooting stars,
sutures our wounds, gaping.

Great is the name of Jehovah;
no other name is found!
The Lord elevates the humble;
throws his foes to the ground.

Make melody, O harp and lyre,
drench the green grass with song!
For he provides for everything
that to himself belongs.

His pleasure is not in the horse
or in strength of man's legs.
But in the ones who fear—who drink
his great love to the dregs.

Zion, extol the awesome name
that strengthens, fortifies;
enforces peace within your gates,
whose manna satisfies.

His precepts pour upon the earth—
words pure and white like snow;
his judgments pelt like hail and ice
as surging waters flow.

He revealed his will in Zion—
his law and his decree;
Jacob's eyes, he opened, all else
closed to the mystery.

Praise the Lord!

Psalm 148
Terzanelle

Praise the Lord from the highest height!
Angels, seraphs, and heavenly host—
his stars chosen to light up the night.

Waters contouring every coast,
sing praise the Lord! Laud his great name—
angels, seraphs, and heavenly host,

his decree shall not be put to shame!
Snow and mist; wind, hail, sea, and fire,
sing praise to the Lord, laud his great name!

Mountains and trees, livestock and brier,
men, women, and kings and princes, fair;
snow and mist; wind, hail, sea and fire—

exalt his great name in song and prayer!
A horn has been raised for all who fear—
men, women, and kings and princes, fair.

To all of his peoples who draw near,
praise the Lord from the highest height!
A horn has been raised for all who fear—
his stars chosen to light up the night.

Psalm 149
Nature Poem

Praise the Lord!
May new songs bloom;
praise him in the garden of our God.
In sod solid, florets bend beneath the breezes,
bowing to their Gardener and Friend.
Labiate leaves leaping—dancing ditties, prancing praises.
Breath of God raises nodes that conduct a symphony
of Scarlet Buglers, Desert Trumpets, Violas, and Lyre Pods.
In God's bosom delight and pleasure rises
as he apprises his glory reflected in their songs.
Melodies ascend like chlorophyll up green throats,
sweet notes rising like seedlings from fertile flower beds.
Bass notes and dark chords rumble,
from the thorny swords of the humble—
music with both bite and beauty like a rose.
Bind Rafflesia with stout vines to trellises of iron;
environ the parasite—with pesticides, embalm. Permit
the Pruner to slit its throat with holy shears
while his ears attune to the singing of his blooms.
He entombs wild weeds and accedes to their decay,
while he grooms the loveliest of his annuals
for his choicest bouquet.

Psalm 150
Trois-par-Huit

Praise the Lord

Praise the name
of the Lord, spread his fame;
praise both his sovereign joy and ire!

Sound the golden trumpets, flaming with holy fire!
Dance with joy; strum the strings of the harp and lyre!

Harmony within clashing discord;
panting praise—one accord:
"Praise the Lord!"

Endnotes

1. Psalm 59 was started by Eileen on 10/2/07. She selected the poetry format (Cycle) and composed the first two lines of stanza one, originally reading: "Save me, O God, from evildoers, See how they wait for me." The remainder of the poem was completed by Vicki on 2/6/2014.

2. Psalm 104 was started by Eileen on 5/20/12. She also worked on the poem on 7/24/12. She also selected the poetry format (Dr. Stella). Eileen composed the first five lines of stanza one (slightly modified by Vicki in the final draft), originally reading: "The Lord is clothed with majesty, in light as with a garment, he makes the clouds his chariot and rides on wind-swept wings. The earth was set by his decree." The remainder of the poem was completed by Vicki 1/30/14.

3. Psalm 98 was modeled after the rhyme scheme and poetic format of Dr. Seuss' book *Oh, the Places You'll Go!*

   The poem is meant to be jubilant and triumphant. I hesitated including the poem in the collection, fearing it would be misinterpreted as irreverent, which is not my intention. Not believing "fear of man" was a good enough reason to omit the poem, I included it and declare with David, "I will become even more undignified than this!" as I cling to the intent of the poem, namely, childlike wonder and awe at the joy of loudly singing praises to our Maker and King—a mandate given to all believers in Matthew 19:14. My prayer is that the poem will be received by its readers with both grace and delight.

4. Psalm 78 was modeled after the poetic format used by J. R. R. Tolkien in his Elder Edda poem, *The Legend of Sigurd and Gudrun.*

5. For sake of consistency and ease of reading, I chose to not capitalize the personal pronouns referring to God (e.g. He, His, Him, etc). This was a literary choice in order to make the flow of each poem easier to read and in no way is intended to call into question either author's full adherence to the biblical view that God, Jesus Christ, and the Holy Spirit are a Triune God worthy of all reverence and worship. My prayer is that this formatting decision will not cause any readers to stumble and will be received with grace and understanding.

Bibliography

Berg, Viola Jacobson. *Pathways for the Poet: Poetry Patterns Explained and Illustrated*. Milford, Mich.: Mott Media, 1977.

Clitheroe, Terry. "The Poets Garret." *The Poets Garret*. N.p., n.d. Web. 02 Feb. 2014. <http://thepoetsgarret.com/>.

Dr. Seuss. *Oh, the Places You'll Go!* London: HarperCollins Children's, 2011.

Tolkien, J. R. R., and Christopher Tolkien. *The Legend of Sigurd and Gudrún*. Boston: Houghton Mifflin Harcourt, 2009.

Index of Poetical Forms

Note: This glossary is a very bare-bones representation of the poetry forms represented within this work. Many of these forms have multiple variations and adaptations and allow for numerous types of rhyme scheme, meter, and syllabification. I intentionally avoided needlessly complicated literary jargon in order to appeal to novice poets unfamiliar with poetry lingo. I highly recommend a poetry handbook to anyone looking to create their own poetry.

Abercrombie
This form consists of any number of four-line stanzas. Line 4 of every stanza ends with a feminine rhyme. The syllable count is 10-8-10-7. The rhyme scheme is *abac dbdc efeg hfhg.*

Acrostic
This form consists of any number of stanzas written in any meter. The first letter of every line, when read vertically, spells out the theme of the poem. The rhyme scheme is *ababab.*

Adagem
This form, a variation of the acrostic, consists of any number of stanzas written in any meter. Unlike the acrostic, which emphasizes the first letter of every line, this form emphasizes the first complete word of every line. When read vertically, the words read as a phrase, sentence, or message.

Ae Freslighe
This Irish form consists of any number of four-line stanzas. Line 1 and line 3 end with a three-syllable word. Line 2 and line 4 end with a two-syllable word. The first word of the poem is also the last word of the poem. Every line contains seven syllables. The rhyme scheme is *abab.*

Alexandrine

This form consists of three, five-line stanzas. The syllable count is 2-4-6-8-2. The rhyme scheme is *abaab cdcdc effef.*

Amphion

This form consists of one, ten-line stanza. The syllable count is 8-3-3-8-3-3-8-3-3-8. Rhyme scheme is *abbaccdeed.*

Apostrophe

This form requires the poet to speak directly to an inanimate object or thing as if they are speaking to another human being.

Arkaham Ballad

This form consists of any number of five-line stanzas. The last line of each stanza becomes the first three feet of the next stanza. The syllable count is 8-6-8-8-6. The rhyme scheme is *xabba.*

Arnold

This form consists of any number of five-line stanzas. The fifth line of each stanza is centered under the previous four. The syllable count is 6-6-6-6-12. The rhyme scheme is *ababc.*

Baccreseize

This form consists of one, twelve-line stanza. Line 1 and line 7 are identical and the last four syllables are repeated as the last four syllables of line 2. Lines 4, 8, and 12 are identical and the full line repeats as the last four syllables of line 5. The syllable count is 8-8-8-4-8-8-8-4-8-8-8-4. The rhyme scheme is *AaxBbxABxxxB.*

Balance

This form consists of three stanzas. Stanza 1 is five lines with a syllable count of 10-8-6-4-2. Stanza 2 is ten lines with a syllable count of 2-4-6-8-10-10-8-6-4-2. Stanza 3 is five lines with a syllable count of 2-4-6-8-10. The first line of the poem is repeated as the final line of the poem. The rhyme scheme is *Abcde edcbaabcde edcbA.*

Balasi Stanza

This form consists of any number of nine-line stanzas. The syllable count is 6-6-7-6-6-7-6-6-7. The rhyme scheme is *aadbbdccd.*

Ballad

This form began as an oral tradition and tended to be songs praising folk legends and heroes. There are no set rules for rhyme scheme, meter, or length.

Ballad Stanza

This form consists of any number of four-line stanzas. The syllable count is 8-6-8-6. The rhyme scheme is *xaxa.*

Ballade

This form consists of three, eight-line stanzas and an envoi (concluding four-line stanza). The last line of every stanza is the same. The rhyme scheme for the stanzas is *ababbcbC.* The rhyme scheme for the envoi is *bcbC.*

Blank Verse

This form consists of any number of unrhymed stanzas. Stanza breaks come at the end of each thought (similar to a paragraph break in prose writing). Blank verse contains run-on lines, which means the end of each line is not necessarily the end of the sentence, but "runs on" to the next line/s of text freely without pause.

Blues Stanza

This Afro-American form consists of any number of three-line stanzas. Line 1 and line 2 end with the same word. Line 3 ends with a word that rhymes. The rhyme scheme is *AAa BBb CCc.*

Blunden

This form consists of any number of six-line stanzas. The syllable count is 8-6-8-8-8-6. The rhyme scheme is *abccab.*

Boutonniere

This form consists of one, thirteen-line stanza. The first two lines of the poem are repeated as the last two lines of the poem. Every line contains seven syllables. The rhyme scheme is *A1A2bbcccbdddA1A2*.

Bridges

This form consists of any number of six-line stanzas. The syllable count is 12-12-4-12-10-4. The four-syllable lines are centered. The rhyme scheme is *aabccb*.

Briolette

This form consists of any number of five-line stanzas. Every line contains eight syllables. The rhyme scheme is *aaabb*.

Bryant

This form consists of any number of four-line stanzas. The syllable count is 6-10-10-6. The short lines are indented. The rhyme scheme is *abab*.

Byr A Thoddaid

This Welsh form consists of any number of four-line stanzas. The tenth syllable (syllable, not word) of Line 3 links to the sixth syllable of line 4 by alliteration, assonance, or secondary rhyme. The last syllable of line 4 links back to the seventh, eighth, or ninth syllable of line 3 by alliteration, assonance, or secondary rhyme. The syllable count is 8-8-10-6.

Casbairdne

This Irish form consists of any number of four-line stanzas. Lines 1 and 3 consonate with lines 2 and 4. There are at least two cross-rhymes in each couplet. In the first couplet, this cross-rhyme does not have to be exact. The final syllable of line 4 alliterates with the preceding stressed word. Every line ends with a three-syllable word. Every line contains seven syllables. The rhyme scheme is *abab*.

Cavatina

This form consists of one, ten-line stanza. The syllable count is 10-4-10-4-10-4-10-4-10-10. The rhyme scheme is *xaxaxbxbcc.*

Chain Verse

This form consists of any number of four-line stanzas. The second line of the first stanza is repeated as the first line of the second stanza. This pattern follows through the entire poem. The first and last lines of the poem are the same. The rhyme scheme is *ABab BCbc CDcd DadA.*

Chant Royal

This French form consists of five, eleven-line stanzas and a five-line envoi. The last line of stanza 1 becomes a refrain and is repeated as the last line of every stanza as well as the last line of the envoi. The rhyme scheme for the stanzas is *ababccddedE.* The rhyme scheme for the envoi is *ddedE.*

Collins Sestet

This form consists of any number of six-line stanzas. Every line contains eight syllables. The rhyme scheme is *aabbcc.*

Complete Couplets

This form consists of any number of two-line stanzas. A couplet is considered "complete" when it expresses a complete thought. The rhyme scheme is *aa bb cc dd.*

Cycle

This form consists of three, four-line stanzas. Line 1 and line 3 of every stanza ends with a feminine rhyme. The syllable count is 9-6-9-6. The rhyme scheme is *abab cbcb dbdb.*

Cyclus

This form consists of one, twelve-line stanza. Line 6 and line 12 are the same. The syllable count is 2-4-6-6-4-2-2-4-6-6-4-2. The rhyme scheme is *xxaxxxxxaxxx.*

Cyhydedd hir

This Welsh form consists of any number of eight-line stanzas. The syllable count is 5-5-5-4-5-5-5-4. The rhyme scheme is *bbbAcccA*.

Decanelle

This form consists of one, ten-line stanza. The odd-numbered lines end with feminine rhymes. The syllable count is 8-7-8-7-8-7-8-7-8-7. The rhyme scheme is *xaxaxaxbxb*.

Decathlon

This form consists of any number of ten-line stanzas. The syllable count is 8-8-4-8-4-8-8-4-10-10. The rhyme scheme is *axbxaccbdd*.

Decuain

This form consists of one, ten-line stanza. Every line contains ten syllables. There are three choices of rhyme scheme: *ababbcbcaa*, *ababbcbcbb*, or *ababbcbccc*.

De La Mare

This form consists of one, eight-line stanza. The lines alternate masculine and feminine endings. Only the masculine endings require rhyme. The syllable count is 8-7-8-4-8-7-8-4. The rhyme scheme is *xaxaxbxb*.

De Tabley

This form consists of three, four-line stanzas. The syllable count is 10-6-10-6. The rhyme scheme is *abab cdcd efef.*

Diatelle

This form consists of one, fifteen-line stanza. The lines are centered on the page so that the poem is shaped like a diamond. The syllable count is 1-2-3-4-6-8-10-12-10-8-6-4-3-2/-1. The rhyme scheme is abbcbccaccbcbba.

Dickson Nocturne
This form consists of one, twelve-line stanza. Lines 3, 7, and 12 are the same. The syllable count is 6-6-4-6-6-6-4-6-6-4-6-4. The rhyme scheme is *aaB cccB ddbdB*.

Dionol
This form consists of one, nine-line stanza. The first eight lines all contain twelve syllables. The final line contains six syllables and should be a repetition of the last six syllables of line 2. The rhyme scheme is *abcddcbab½*.

Dixdeux
This form consists of any number of three-line stanzas. The syllable count is 10-10-2. There is no rhyme scheme.

Dizain
This form consists of one, ten-line stanza. Every line contains ten syllables. (Eight syllables is also accepted). The rhyme scheme is *ababbccdcd*.

Donne
This form consists of any number of six-line stanzas. The syllable count is 10-10-10-10-8-4. The rhyme scheme is *ababab*.

Dorsimbra
This form consists of three, four-line stanzas. The first stanza contains ten-syllable lines, using the rhyme scheme *abab*. The second stanza is written in free verse. The third stanza contains ten-syllable lines and does not rhyme. The first and last lines of the poem are the same. The rhyme scheme is *Abab xxxx xxxA*.

Douzet
This form consists of three, twelve-line stanzas. Every line contains 10 syllables. The rhyme scheme for stanza 1 and 2 is *abba cddc*. The rhyme scheme for stanza 3 is *abcd*.

Dowson

This form consists of two, four-line stanzas. Lines 1 and 3 end with feminine rhymes. Lines 2 and 4 end with masculine rhymes. The syllable count is 11-6-11-4. The rhyme scheme is *abab cdcd*.

Dr. Seuss

This form is patterned after the writing style of American children's book author, Theodor Seuss Geisel (a.k.a. Dr. Seuss.)

Dr. Stella

This form consists of any number of eight-line stanzas. Line 2 and line 6 end with feminine rhymes. The syllable count is 8-6-8-6-8-6-8-6. The rhyme scheme is *abcdabcd*.

Duni

This form consists of any number of seven-line stanzas that conform to a very stringent meter and rhyme scheme for each line (see below). Line 6 introduces a shift in thought that should complement or strengthen the message laid out in lines 1 through 5. They rhyme scheme is *abcdcba*.

> Line 1: dactyl, two trochees, iamb
> Line 2: three iambs
> Line 3: trochee, anapest, two iambs
> Line 4: three iambs
> Line 5: three iambs
> Line 6: four iambs
> Line 7: iamb, anapest, iamb

Duodora

This form consists of two, seven-line stanzas. Line 1 of the first stanza is repeated again as line 1 of the second stanza. The syllable count is 4-6-5-5-5-10-10. The rhyme scheme is *Axxxxxb Axxxxxb*.

Elder Edda

This Old Norse form is an epic-like, historical narrative that proclaims the heroic deeds of a mythical or legendary character. The form follows a very rigid rule set of meter, assonance, and alliteration. The poem included in this volume utilizes the eight-line, "fornyroislag" stanza. Every line consists of a minimum of four syllables, but can also have five, or occasionally (used sparingly) six. Every other line must assonate or alliterate with the previous line, but the repetition should not fall on the last "lift" of the line. Similar to Anglo-Saxon poetry, this form incorporates lays and kennings; a lay being a side story or apparent "tangent" from the main theme of the poem, and a kenning being a descriptive compound word, connected by a hyphen, that replaces a common noun with a thought picture. For a far more thorough description, see Christopher Tolkien's "Introduction" section of J. R. R. Tolkien's book, "The Legend of Sigurd & Gudrun."

Elegy

An elegy is similar to a eulogy given at a funeral; however, an elegy is not limited to the subject of a person. It could be about a place, an experience, a feeling, or any topic that is weighing heavy on the heart of a poet. The tone of the poem is typically sad or mournful and pertains to some form of loss. There is no set meter or rhyme scheme.

Empat Empat

This Malaysian form consists of four, four-line stanzas. The first line of the first stanza repeats in every stanza as the second line of the second stanza, the third line of the third stanza, and the forth line of the forth stanza. Rhyme schemes include, but are not limited to, *Aabb aAcc, or Abab cAcb, or Abba cAac or Axyz, dAfg.*

Enclosed Triplet

This form consists of any number of three-line stanzas. The rhyme scheme is *aba bcb cdc ded*, etc.

English Quintain
This form is a five-line stanza that acts as a building block for several other poetry forms (e.g. ballad, sonnetina cinque, sonnet, etc.). There is no set measure or foot. The rhyme scheme is *ababb*.

Envelope Stanza
This form consists of any number of four-line stanzas. Every line contains eight syllables. The rhyme scheme is *abba*.

Etheree
This form consists of one, ten-line stanza that increases by one syllable per line. Line 1 is one syllable, line 2 is two syllables, line 3 is three syllables, etc. The very last word of the poem should not be a preposition or a conjunction. There is no rhyme scheme.

Fjorton
This form was created especially for this volume of poetry. The form consists of seven couplets that contain both a head and a tail rhyme for a total of fourteen rhymes. (Thus the title of the poetry form. Fjorton is the Swedish word for fourteen). Any number of internal rhymes are also encouraged, but not required. No specific syllable count is required, but long and short lines alternate. The rhyme scheme is *aa bb cc dd ee ff gg*.

Fletcher
This form consists of two, eight-line stanzas. Line 1 and line 3 of each stanza end with a feminine rhyme. The syllable count is 10-4-10-4-10-4-4-10. The rhyme scheme is *ababcdcd efefghgh*.

Ghazal
This Moslem form consists of any number of two-line stanzas. The last word of line 1 repeats as the last word used in line 2 of every stanza. The rhyme scheme is *AA bA cA*.

Gilbert

This form consists of any number of seven-line stanzas. The syllable count is 8-6-8-8-8-6-8. The rhyme scheme is *xabbacc.*

Goethe Stanza

This form consists of any number of four-line stanzas. Line 1 and line 2 are double spaced; line 2 and line 3 are single spaced; and line 3 and line 4 are double spaced. There is no set meter. The rhyme scheme is *abab.*

Half Measure

This form consists of any number of four-line stanzas. Every line contains six syllables. The rhyme scheme is either *abab* or *abcb.*

Herrick

The form consists of any number of four-line stanzas. Line 1 and line 3 end with masculine rhymes. Line 2 and line 4 end with feminine rhymes. They syllable count is 8-7-8-7. The rhyme scheme is *abab cdcd efef ghgh.*

Hexaduad

This form consists of one, twelve-line stanza. Line 1 is repeated as line 12 and line 2 is repeated as line 11. The syllable count is 2-6-8-4-6-4-4-6-4-8-6-2. The rhyme scheme is *AAbbccddeeAA.*

Hymnal Measure

This form consists of any number of four-line stanzas. The syllable count is 8-6-8-6. The rhyme scheme is *abab.*

Kipling

This form consists of any number of four-line stanzas. Line 1 and line 3 contain an internal rhyme. The syllable count is 14-7-14-7. The rhyme scheme is *(aa)b(cc)b.*

Kloang

This Thai form consists of three, four-line stanzas. Every line contains a space between the fifth and sixth syllables. The syllable count is 7-7-7-9. The rhyme scheme intertwines throughout the entire poem. Syllable 5 of line 1 rhymes with the final syllable of line 2 and syllable 5 of line 4. Syllable 5 of line 2 and line 3 rhymes with the last syllable of line 1. The end word of line 3 and line 4 rhyme.

Kyrielle

This French form consists of any number of four-line stanzas. The last line of the first stanza repeats as the last line of every stanza. There are eight syllables per line. The rhyme scheme is *aabb ccdd eeff*.

Latova

This form consists of two, nine-line stanzas. There are seven syllables per line. The rhyme scheme is *abbcccbaa deefffedd*.

Laurel

This form consists of any number of six-line stanzas. Line 2 and line 6 are indented. The last word of line 1 in stanza 1 and stanza two rhyme. (If there are more than two stanzas, line 1 in stanza 3 and stanza 4 rhyme, etc.). The syllable count is 8-6-8-8-8-6. The rhyme scheme is *abcccb adeeed fghhhg fijjji*.

Lavelle

This form consists of six stanzas. Stanza 1, 5 and 6 are couplets (two lines) and stanza 2, 3 and 4 are tercets (three lines). The first and last stanza has the same end rhyme. Every line contains eight syllables. The rhyme scheme is *aa bbb ccc ddd ee ff*.

Logolilt

This form consists of two, six-line stanzas. The syllable count is 8-4-2-8-4-2. The rhyme scheme is *aabccb ddeffe*.

Louise
This form consists of any number of four-line stanzas. Line 1 and line 3 end with a feminine rhyme. The syllable count is 10-10-10-4. The rhyme scheme is *xaxa xbxb*.

Luc Bat
This Vietnamese form alternates between lines of six syllables and eight syllables. The last syllable of the first odd-numbered line (line 1) rhymes with the sixth syllable of the first even-numbered line (line 2); the eighth syllable of the first even-numbered line (line 2) rhymes with the sixth syllable of the next odd line (line 3). This pattern continues throughout the rest of the poem. There is no set length; however, the final even-numbered line links back to rhyme with the first line of the poem. The first and the last word of the poem should be the same word.

LuVailean Sonnet
This form consists of one, fourteen-line stanza. The syllable count is 10-4-10-4-10-4-10-4-10-4-10-4-10-10. The rhyme scheme is *ababcdcdefefgg*.

Lyrelle
This form consists of two to four, four-line stanzas. The syllable count is 4-6-8-10. The rhyme scheme is *abab cdcd*.

Lyric
This form is broadly defined. There is no set meter, length, or rhyme scheme (though a rhyme scheme of some kind is typically assumed). Lyrics tend to have a rhythm that mimics song lyrics.

Marianne
This form consists of any number of five-line stanzas. All of the lines are centered on the page. The syllable count is 4-6-8-4-2. The rhyme scheme is *axaxa*.

Mathlish

The form combines two, two-line Persian mathnawis with two, three-line Arabian mathnawis and a concluding quatrain (four-line stanza) that acts as a volta. The rhyme scheme for the stanzas are *aa bbb cc ddd*. The three rhyme scheme options for the volta are: Sicilian (*abab*), Italian (*abba*), or Spanish (*aabb*).

Mathnawi

This Persian form consists of any number of eleven-syllable couplets (occasionally ten). The rhyme scheme is *aa bb cc dd*.

Medallion

This form consists of one, nine-line stanza. Every line is centered on the page. The syllable count is 4-7-8-7-9-10-9-7-4. The rhyme scheme is *xabccbadd*.

Metric Pyramid

This form consists of one, eight-line stanza. The syllable count is 2-4-6-8-10-12-14-16. The rhyme scheme is *abbaabba*.

Monchielle Stanza

This form consists of four, five-line stanzas. The first line of the first stanza is repeated as the first line of all subsequent stanzas. The rhyme scheme is *xxaxa*.

Muzdawidj

This Arabic form is a variation of the Persian mathnawi. Unlike the mathnawi (which is comprised of couplets) this form is written in triplets. The rhyme scheme is *aaa bbb ccc*.

Nature Poem

This form consists of any number of stanzas, written in any meter, in any rhyme scheme. Michael Bugeja lays out ten types of nature poems in his book, "The Art and Craft of Poetry." The type used within this volume is the "nature as metaphor" form.

Neville
This form consists of one, seven-line stanza. The syllable count is 8-6-6-8-6-6-8. The rhyme scheme is *abbacca.*

Novelinee
This form consists of any number of nine-line stanzas. The last line of the final stanza ends with a variation of the first line of the first stanza. Every line contains ten syllables. The rhyme scheme is *ababcdcdd.*

Octave
This form consists of one, eight-line stanza. The rhyme schemes include, but are not limited to, *ababcdcd, aaabcccb,* and *ababccab.*

Octodil
This form consists of one, eight-line stanza. The syllable count is 4-4-6-6-8-8-6-6. No rhyme scheme is required.

Octosyllabic Couplets
This form consists of any number of couplets. The syllable count is 8-8. The rhyme scheme is *aa bb cc dd*, etc.

Ottava Rima
This Italian form consists of one, eight-line stanza. The rhyme scheme is *abababcc.*

Pantoum
This Malaysian form consists of any number of four-line stanzas. Line 2 and line 4 of the first stanza are repeated as line 1 and line 3 of the second stanza. This pattern then repeats with line 2 and 4 of the second stanza repeating as line 1 and 3 of the third stanza, etc. Line 2 and line 4 of the final stanza repeat line 1 and 3 of the first stanza. Every line contains eight syllables. The rhyme scheme is *aBaB BcBc CdCd DeDe EAEA.*

Pleiades

This form consists of one, seven-line stanza. The title of the poem and the first word in every line all begin with the same letter of the alphabet. No set meter, syllable count, or rhyme scheme is required.

Poulter's Measure

This form consists of any number of four-line stanzas. The syllable count is 12-14-12-14. No rhyme scheme is required.

Quatern

This form consists of four, four-line stanzas. The first line of the first stanza repeats in every stanza as the second line of the second stanza, the third line of the third stanza, and the last line of the last stanza. Every line contains eight syllables. No rhyme scheme is required.

Quintanelle

This form consists of any number of five-line stanzas. The syllable count is 10-10-4-6-10. The rhyme scheme is *aabbb*.

Quintilla

This form consists of any number of five-line stanzas. Every line contains eight syllables. The rhyme scheme varies, but only two consecutive lines can rhyme (e.g. *aabba* or *abbaa*).

Repete

This form consists of one, eight-line and one, six-line stanza. Line 1 and line 2 are repeated as line 7 and line 8 and again as lines 13 and 14. The wording of the refrain does not have to be identical. Every line contains eight syllables. The rhyme scheme is *ABababAB ababAB*.

Retournello

This form consists of any number of four-line stanzas. Line 1 and line 4 of each stanza repeat but do not have to be identical. The syllable count is 4-6-8-4. The rhyme scheme is *abba*.

Retruecano (Glosa)
This Spanish form consists of any number of stanzas and begins with a texto. The texto should summarize the theme of the poem. The number of lines in the texto determines the number of stanzas. (e.g. A two-line texto will have two stanzas; a three-line texto will have three stanzas, etc.). Line 1 of the texto will be repeated as the final line of the first stanza. Line 2 of the texto will be repeated as the final line of the second stanza, etc. The stanzas can be any number of lines but are typically in multiples of two. The rhyme scheme is *aabbcc*.

Rhopalic Verse
This form does not have any set rules pertaining to length, meter, number of syllables, or rhyme scheme. The only requirement is that the first word of every line has one syllable, the second word has two syllables, the third word has three syllables, etc.

Rhymed Cinquain
This form consists of any number of five-line stanzas. The syllable count is 6-5-6-6-12. The rhyme scheme is *ababb*.

Rime Couee
This French form consists of any number of six-line stanzas. The syllable count is 8-8-6-8-8-6. The rhyme scheme is *aabaab*.

Rondeau
This French form consists of three stanzas, made up of fifteen lines. The refrain appears as line 1 of stanza 1 and also as the final line of stanza 2 and 3. (The refrain can be either a full or partial repetition. Every line contains ten syllables. The rhyme scheme is *Rabba aabR aabbaR*.

Rondeau Redouble
This form consists of six, four-line stanzas. The final stanza has a fifth line, which is a half-line refrain of the first half of stanza 1, line 1. All of the lines in the first stanza are repeated (line 1 is the last line of stanza 2; line 2 is the last line of stanza 3; line 3 is the last line of

stanza 4; and line 4 is the last line of stanza 5). Every line contains ten syllables. The rhyme scheme is *ABa-1b-1 babA abaB baba-1 abab-1 babaA½*.

Rondel

This French form consists of fourteen lines broken into two stanzas. Stanza 1 is eight lines and stanza 2 is six lines. Line 1 and line 2 are repeated as line 7 and line 8 in the final couplet of both stanzas. Every line contains ten syllables. The rhyme scheme is *ABbaabAB abbaAB*.

Rondine

This form consists of two stanzas. The first stanza contains seven lines and the second stanza contains five lines. The final line of both stanzas is a refrain, which is a repetition of the first phrase of line 1. The syllable count is 10-10-10-10-10-4-10-10-10-10-4. The rhyme scheme is *RbbaabR½ abbaR½*.

Rosemary

This form consists of one, twelve-line stanza. Every line contains ten syllables. The "c" and "e" lines are indented. The rhyme scheme is *aabccbdeedff*.

Roundelay

This form consists of any number of four-line stanzas. The rhyme scheme is *ccbA ddbA eebA*.

Rubaiyat

This Persian form consists of any number of four-line stanzas. Lines 1, 2, and 4 rhyme and the end rhyme of line 3 is carried over to lines 1, 2, and 4 of the next stanza. This pattern then repeats. Every line contains ten syllables. The rhyme scheme is *aaba*.

Russell

This form contains of three, four-line stanzas. The syllable count is 10-10-10-6. The short lines are indented. The rhyme scheme is *abab cdcd efef*.

Sacred Signia
This form consists of any number of ten-line stanzas. They syllable count is 10-4-10-4-10-4-10-10-10-10. The rhyme scheme is *ababcbccaa*.

Saraband
This Asian form consists of two, seven-line stanzas. Every line contains eight syllables. The rhyme scheme is *axabcbc dddeeff*.

Septilla (Spanish Septet)
This form consists of any number of seven-line stanzas. The syllable count is 8-8-8-8-8-8-8. The rhyme scheme is either *aabccba* or *abbacca*.

Serena
This form consists of one, eleven-line stanza. Lines 1 and 2 are repeated as lines 9 and 10. Lines 3 through 8 have both head rhymes (first word in line) and tail rhymes (last word in line). The head rhymes follow a rhyme scheme of *AAbbccddAAx*. The end rhymes follow a rhyme scheme of *ABcxccddABb*.

Sestennelle
This form consists of three, six-line stanzas. The syllable count is 4-6-10-4-6-10. The rhyme scheme is *aabccb ddeffe gghiih*.

Sestet
This form consists of one, six-line stanza. The rhyme scheme can be *aabbcc, ababcc, aabccb, aaabbb*.

Sestina
This form consists of seven stanzas. Six, six-line stanzas and a closing three-line stanza.

The six end words used at the end of every line in the first stanza are carried through the rest of the poem. The same six words are used at the end of the line in every stanza, but in a different order each time. The poem does not have to rhyme, but can if the poet so chooses. The order for the six end words in the six successive stanzas are as follows:

Stanza One:	1, 2, 3, 4, 5, 6
Stanza Two:	6, 1, 5, 2, 4, 3
Stanza Three:	3, 6, 4, 1, 2, 5
Stanza Four:	5, 3, 2, 6, 1, 4
Stanza Five:	4, 5, 1, 3, 6, 2
Stanza Six:	2, 4, 6, 5, 3, 1
Half Stanza:	2, 4, 6

Terminal words 1, 3, 5, are used near the beginning or center of the half-stanza lines.

Sevenelle

This form consists of two or more seven-line stanzas. Line 6 and line 7 are the same in every stanza. Every line contains eight syllables. The rhyme scheme is *aabbbCC ddeeeCC*.

Sonnet

This Italian form consists of one, fourteen-line stanza. The main idea of the poem is laid out in lines 1 through 8. Lines 9 through 14 build the main idea to its conclusion. Sonnets also generally contain a *volta* (or turn). The volta usually appears in line 8, but this can vary. The volta should shift the direction of the poem into a different direction. Every line contains ten syllables. The rhyme scheme is dependent upon what type of sonnet is being written.

Sonnetina Cinque

This form consists of two, five-line stanzas. The first stanza makes a statement. The second stanza makes a contra statement. There is no set meter or rhyme scheme.

Spenserian Stanza

This form consists of one, nine-line stanza. There is typically a caesura (break or pause) after the first three feet of the poem. Lines 1 through 8 contain ten syllables. Line 9 contains twelve syllables. The rhyme scheme is *ababbcbcc*

Standard Habbie

This form consists of any number of six-line stanzas. The syllable count is 8-8-8-6-8-6. The rhyme scheme is *aaabab.*

Star Sevlin

This form consists of one, seven-line stanza. The lines are centered on the page to look like a star. The syllable count is 4-6-8-6-8-6-4. The rhyme scheme is *abbcaca.*

Stave Stanza

This form consists of any number of six-line stanzas. The last word of line 5 is the same last word in line 5 of every stanza. Line 6 is a refrain, repeated as line 6 of every stanza. The rhyme scheme is *aabbcC ddeecC ffggcC.*

Stellar

This form consists of three, eight-line stanzas. The fifth and sixth lines of each stanza have feminine endings. The syllable count is 8-8-8-8-9-9-4-8. The rhyme scheme is *ababccdd efefgghh ijijkkll.*

Strambotto Romagnuolo

This Italian form consists of any number of eight-line stanzas. Every line contains eleven syllables. There are three rhyme schemes:

Siciliano	*abababab*
Toscano	*ababab cc*
Romagnuolo	*ababccdd*

Swannet

This form consists of one, fourteen-line stanza. Line 1 and line 4 repeat as line 13 and line 14. Every line contains ten syllables. The rhyme scheme is A1bbA2cddceffeA1A2.

Sweetbriar

This form consists of two, six-line stanzas. The syllable count is 4-4-6-4-4-6. The rhyme scheme is xxaxxa.

Tanka

This form consists of one, five-line stanza. The syllable count is 5-7-5-7-7. No rhyme scheme is required.

Tennyson

This form consists of three, five-line stanzas. The title of the poem is also used as a refrain that is repeated as the opening phrase of line1 and the last line (line 5) of all three stanzas. The syllable count is 10-10-10-10-4. The rhyme scheme is abbaR cddcR effeR.

Tercets with Identical Refrain

This form consists of any number of four-line stanzas. Line 4 of every stanza is the same. The syllable count is 10-10-10-6. The rhyme scheme is aaaR bbbR cccR.

Terzanelle

This form consists of six stanzas composed of five, three-line stanzas and a concluding four-line stanza. The second line of every stanza is repeated as the final line of the following stanza. Three of the four lines in the final stanza are repeated. Line 2 is a repeat of stanza 1, line 1. Line 3 is a repeat of stanza 5, line 2. Line 4 is a repeat of stanza 1, line 3. The rhyme scheme for the three-line stanzas is aba bcb cdc ded efe. The rhyme scheme for the final stanza is fafa.

Terza Rima

This Italian form consists of four, three-line stanzas and a concluding couplet. Line 2 sets the rhyme scheme for line 1 and line 3 of the next stanza. This pattern then repeats in all subsequent stanzas. Every line contains ten syllables. The rhyme scheme is *aba bcb cdc ded ee.*

Than Bauk

This Asian form consists of any number of three-line stanzas. The rhyme scheme for this form creates a "staircase" effect. Line 1 contains an end rhyme. The word at the end of line 1 rhymes with a word in the middle of line 2 and also with a word at the beginning of line 3. The last word in line 3 then acts as the end rhyme in line 1 of the next stanza. The pattern then repeats throughout the rest of the poem. Every line contains four syllables.

Trench

This form is consists of any number of five-line stanzas. The syllable count is 10-10-4-10-6. The rhyme scheme is *axbab.*

Triad

This form consists of three stanzas. Stanzas 1 and 3 contain eight lines and a refrain. Stanza 2 contains 5 lines and a refrain. The refrain (which includes an internal rhyme) is also used as the title of the poem. Every line contains eight syllables, except for the refrain, which contains four syllables. The rhyme scheme is *xxxaxabA xxxabA xxxaxabA.*

Trijan Refrain

This form consists of three, nine-line stanzas. Traditionally, line 1 is repeated as a refrain as line 1 of all three stanzas. This rule has since been omitted and a different opening line for each stanza can be used. In every stanza, the first four syllables of line 5 are repeated as a double-refrain in lines 7 and 8. The syllable count is 8-6-8-6-8-8-4-4-8. The rhyme scheme is *abab(RRRR)cc(RRRR)(RRRR)c.*

Triolet

This form consists of any number of eight-line stanzas. Line 1 repeats in line 4 and line 7. Line 2 is repeated in line 8. Every line contains eleven syllables. The rhyme scheme is *ABaAabAB*.

Trois-par-Huit

This form consists of three, eight-line stanzas. The last line of the poem (also the poem's title) should summarize the meaning of the poem. All of the lines are centered. The stanzas can either be broken up into lines of 3-3-2 or 3-2-3. The syllable count is 3-6-9-12-12-9-6-3. The rhyme scheme is *aab bbc cc* or *aab bb ccc*.

Veltanelle

This form consists of one, two, or three, six-line stanzas. The syllable count 10-6-10-6-10-10. The rhyme scheme is *ababcc dedeff ghghii*.

Villanelle

This form consists of five, three-line stanzas with a concluding four-line stanza. Line 1 and line 3 of the first stanza are repeated several times throughout the poem. Every line contains eight syllables. The rhyme scheme is *A1bA2 abA1 abA2 abA1 abA2 abA1A2*.

Virelet

This French form consists of any number of four-line stanzas. The last word of each stanza sets the opening rhyme of the next stanza. The last line of the final stanza should rhyme with the last word in the first line of the poem. There is no set syllable count but it is assumed that every other line alternates with a long and a short line. The rhyme scheme is *abab bcbc cdcd dada*.

Wavelet

This form consists of one, twelve-line stanza. The syllable count is 5-5-8-8-8-5-5-8-8-8-5-5. The five-syllable lines are indented. The rhyme scheme is *aabcbddeceff*.

Wordsworth Sestet

This form consists of any number of six-line stanzas. Every line contains ten syllables. The rhyme scheme is *abbcac*.

Wreathed Quatrain

This English/Welsh form consists of any number of four-line stanzas. The form utilizes both internal and end rhymes. The internal rhyme can be anywhere in the first half of the following line. The word can either be a rhyme or the exact same word used again. There is no internal rhyme in the first line of every stanza. The rhyme scheme for the internal rhyme is *xaba*. The rhyme scheme for the tail rhyme is *abab*.

ZaniLa Rhyme

This form consists of three or more four-line stanzas. Line 3 contains an internal rhyme and the line is repeated as line 3 of every stanza but with the two phrases of the internal rhyme swapped in alternating stanzas. The syllable count is 9-7-9-9. The rhyme scheme is *xa(BC)a xd(CB)d xe(BC)e xf(CB)f*.

Zanze

This form consists of four, four-line stanzas. The first line of stanza 1 repeats (in part) as line 1 of all subsequent stanzas. Stanza 2, line 1 repeats the first six syllables of stanza 1, line 1. Stanza 3, line 1 repeats the first four syllables of stanza 1, line 1. Stanza 4, line 1 repeats the first two syllables of stanza 1, line 1. The first line of stanza 1 is repeated as the final line of the poem. The syllable count is 8-8-8-8-6-6-6-6-4-4-4-4-2-4-6-8. The rhyme scheme is *Abab cdcd efef gagA*.

Zenith

This form, of no set length or meter, is written in units of six lines (or multiples thereof). Masculine end rhymes are rhymed with masculine words and feminine end rhymes are rhymed with feminine words. The rhyme scheme is *abcabc defdef ghighi*.

Author Index

PSALM	POETRY FORM	DATE WRITTEN	AUTHOR
1	Ottava Rima	1/23/2001	Eileen
2	Adagem	1/24/2001	Eileen
3	Bridges	1/25/2001	Eileen
4	Dionol	2/2/2001	Eileen
5	Rondel	2/3/2001	Eileen
6	Dowson	2/10/2001	Eileen
7	Zanze	Unknown	Eileen
8	Lyrelle	2/7/1997	Eileen
9	Villanelle	2/20/2001	Eileen
10	Stellar	2/20/2001	Eileen
11	Cavatina	2/20/2001	Eileen
12	Sevenelle	Unknown	Eileen
13	Octave	2/13/2001	Eileen
14	De Tabley	5/21/2001	Eileen
15	Spenserian Stanza	2/21/2001	Eileen
16	Russell	9/17/2001	Eileen
17	Arkaham Ballad	10/22/2001	Eileen
18	Chant Royal	4/23/2003	Eileen
19	Sonnet	1/29/1997	Eileen
20	Dorsimbra	11/4/2003	Eileen
21	Quatern	Unknown	Eileen
22	Sestina	Unknown	Eileen
23	Quintanelle	1/11/2002	Eileen
24	Marianne	Unknown	Eileen
25	Sestennelle	7/10/2003	Eileen
26	Octodil	7/19/2003	Eileen
27	Veltanelle	7/10/2003	Eileen

28	Octosyllabic Couplets	8/3/2003	Eileen
29	Terza Rima	8/10/2003	Eileen
30	Duodora	8/11/2003	Eileen
31	Arnold	5/14/2005	Eileen
32	Chain Verse	6/2/2005	Eileen
33	Herrick	6/3/2005	Eileen
34	Acrostic	6/4/2005	Eileen
35	Latova	6/21/2005	Eileen
36	Sacred Signia	6/23/2005	Eileen
37	Lavelle	6/30/2005	Eileen
38	LuVailean Sonnet	7/1/2005	Eileen
39	Tercets with Identical Refrain	8/16/2007	Eileen
40	Abercrombie	7/5/2005	Eileen
41	Hexaduad	7/7/2005	Eileen
42	Apostrophe	7/16/2005	Eileen
43	De La Mare	8/8/2005	Eileen
44	Donne	2/22/2006	Eileen
45	Amphion	3/10/2006	Eileen
46	Tennyson	7/31/1998	Eileen
47	Tanka	8/13/2005	Eileen
48	Balance	3/13/2006	Eileen
49	Medallion	3/23/2006	Eileen
50	Triad	4/4/2006	Eileen
51	Ballade	10/13/2006	Eileen
52	Louise	10/17/2006	Eileen
53	Trench	5/28/2007	Eileen
54	Retournello	7/12/2013	Vicki
55	Rondeau	6/1/2007	Eileen
56	Swannet	8/2/2013	Vicki
57	Decannelle	7/19/2007	Eileen
58	Logolilt	6/9/2007	Eileen
59	Cycle	10/2/2007	Vicki
60	Rime Couee	10/3/2013	Vicki
61	Balasi Stanza	10/4/2013	Vicki

62	Kipling	7/30/2013	Vicki
63	Cyclus	10/12/2007	Eileen
64	Goethe Stanza	8/4/2013	Vicki
65	Retruecano (Glosa)	10/13/2013	Vicki
66	Pantoum	11/9/2008	Eileen
67	Blunden	11/10/2008	Eileen
68	Ballad	11/14/2008	Eileen
69	Rondeau Redouble	7/4/2013	Vicki
70	Bryant	4/15/2009	Eileen
71	Repete	5/27/2009	Eileen
72	Septilla (Spanish Septet)	12/8/2013	Vicki
73	Wreathed Quatrain	8/5/2013	Vicki
74	Mathnawi	11/18/2013	Vicki
75	Monchielle Stanza	10/16/2013	Vicki
76	Novelinee	11/19/2013	Vicki
77	Elegy	6/22/2013	Vicki
78	Elder Edda	12/13/2013	Vicki
79	Blank Verse	11/27/2013	Vicki
80	Trijan Refrain	8/7/2013	Vicki
81	Zenith	10/19/2006	Eileen
82	Sestet	4/2/2011	Vicki
83	Rondine	12/7/2013	Vicki
84	Rosemary	3/6/1997	Eileen
85	Cyhydedd hir	11/20/2013	Vicki
86	Half Measure	8/8/2013	Vicki
87	Dickson Nocturne	5/28/2013	Vicki
88	Luc Bat	7/21/2013	Vicki
89	English Quintain	1/12/2014	Vicki
90	Muzdawidj	9/25/2013	Vicki
91	Dixdeux	7/23/2013	Vicki
92	Empat Empat	1/7/2014	Vicki
93	Fletcher	6/3/2007	Eileen
94	Enclosed Triplet	11/27/2013	Vicki
95	Sonnetina Cinque	1/21/2014	Vicki

96	Kyrielle	5/29/2012	Eileen
97	Douzet	2/23/1997	Eileen
98	Dr. Seuss	1/22/1014	Vicki
99	Standard Habbie	8/2/2013	Vicki
100	Baccreseize	5/8/1992	Eileen
101	Strambotto Romagnuolo	10/22/2013	Vicki
102	Byr A Thoddaid	7/22/2013	Vicki
103	Lyric	6/9/2013	Vicki
104	Dr. Stella	7/24/2012	Vicki
105	Wordsworth Sestet	1/19/2014	Vicki
106	Rubaiyat	1/20/2014	Vicki
107	Blues Stanza	1/21/2014	Vicki
108	Decathlon	7/8/2011	Eileen
109	Stave Stanza	11/19/2013	Vicki
110	Dizain	4/21/2013	Vicki
111	Quintilla	12/17/2013	Vicki
112	Envelope Stanza	8/17/2011	Eileen
113	Ghazal	11/15/2013	Vicki
114	Sweetbriar	7/23/2009	Eileen
115	Boutonniere	7/24/2009	Eileen
116	Duni	11/12/2011	Eileen
117	Etheree	4/7/2013	Vicki
118	Laurel	6/8/2013	Vicki
119	22 Complete Couplets	7/4/2005	Eileen
120	Neville	6/11/2013	Vicki
121	Metric Pyramid	6/11/2013	Vicki
122	Wavelet	4/22/2014	Vicki
123	Hymnal Measure	8/7/2013	Vicki
124	Ae Freslighe	10/18/2013	Vicki
125	Decuain	8/10/2013	Vicki
126	Alexandrine	5/23/2013	Vicki
127	Pleiades	11/4/2013	Vicki
128	Than Bauk	11/4/2013	Vicki
129	Serena	6/13/2013	Vicki

130	Fjorton	6/30/2013	Vicki
131	Rhopalic Verse	6/13/2013	Vicki
132	Diatelle	12/19/2013	Vicki
133	Roundelay	10/23/2013	Vicki
134	Star Sevlin	6/13/2013	Vicki
135	Casbairdne	12/20/2013	Vicki
136	Triolet	10/29/2013	Vicki
137	Kloang	4/7/2013	Vicki
138	ZaniLa Rhyme	10/24/2013	Vicki
139	Collins Sestet	12/18/2013	Vicki
140	Gilbert	6/15/2013	Vicki
141	Mathlish	11/18/2013	Vicki
142	Rhymed Cinquain	5/18/2013	Vicki
143	Virelet	6/15/2013	Vicki
144	Poulter's Measure	7/28/2013	Vicki
145	Saraband	11/15/2013	Vicki
146	Briolette	7/2/2013	Vicki
147	Ballad Stanza	1/6/2014	Vicki
148	Terzanelle	7/9/2013	Vicki
149	Nature Poem	10/24/2013	Vicki
150	Trois-par-Huit	7/4/2013	Vicki

About the Author

Eileen Anderson, wife of Jeff Anderson for forty-seven years, and mother of two adult children, was living in Lakeville, MN at the time of her death in March 2013. Eileen began writing at the age of eight when her first short story, "Betty Jean Runs Away" was published in her elementary school newsletter. Since that time, Eileen had a variety of personal experience articles, devotionals, poetry, music, puzzles, Bible studies, curriculum, and interviews published in magazines such as Guideposts, Sunday Digest, Home Life, Purpose, Discoveries, Keys For Kids, as well as devotionals in My Turn To Care, a book for caregivers, and several personal commentaries in the Collegiate Devotional Bible.

Eileen's daughter, Vicki Anderson, attended University of Northwestern in St. Paul, MN where she obtained a bachelor's in English with a Writing Emphasis. Vicki has had articles published in Pray! and Susie magazines. Vicki currently lives in Pennsylvania.

CPSIA information can be obtained at www.ICGtesting.com
Printed in the USA
BVOW04s0045220714

359975BV00001B/4/P